Remarkability

You're Not Invisible;

Don't Let Your Brand Be Either

By Ginger Rockey-Johnson

Remarkability

You're Not Invisible; Don't Let Your Brand Be Either

By Ginger Rockey-Johnson

Copyright 2014

All Rights Reserved. No part of this book may be reproduced by any mechanical, photographic, or electronic process, or in any form of phonographic recording; nor may it be stored in a retrieval system, transmitted or otherwise copied for public or private use--- other than for (fair use) as brief quotation embodied in articles and reviews---without prior written permission of the author.

ISBN-13: 978-1502574817

ISBN-10: 1502574810

Remarkability

You're Not Invisible;

Don't Let Your Brand Be Either

By Ginger Rockey-Johnson

Remarkability

You're Not Invisible; Don't Let Your Brand Be Either

By Ginger Rockey-Johnson

Copyright 2014

All Rights Reserved. No part of this book may be reproduced by any mechanical, photographic, or electronic process, or in any form of phonographic recording; nor may it be stored in a retrieval system, transmitted or otherwise copied for public or private use--- other than for (fair use) as brief quotation embodied in articles and reviews---without prior written permission of the author.

ISBN-13: 978-1502574817

ISBN-10: 1502574810

Dedication

This book is dedicated to the tireless, passionate, most real people I know, small business owners of the world.

To the coaches and consultants I have been honored to meet and work with over the years, who want to grow into their passion and out of being the technical slave of the marketing & technology world.

To the wedding professionals who thrive on delivering the most amazing experiences of a lifetime to brides and grooms everywhere.

To the executives who were laid off in the economic downturn and found themselves stepping out in faith to build a business so they could have a legacy for their family.

To the single moms who needed to earn extra income to support their children's future dreams while remembering they had one of their own.

Special dedications to a few people in my life who inspire me and push me to keep moving forward.

To the hero in my life, my mom, Billie Borton. She is my inspiration, my treasure, my friend, she is the most brilliant woman in life, in spirit, dedication, and tireless energy. Even though she is not close to me geographically she is still my hero. To my daughter Cheyenne, a pinnacle of loyalty, friendship, and a blossoming young woman, who even in her young age manages to keep her mom in line. She is one of my "Why's" in life, my partner in fun, a blessing of my life that God knew I needed. She is a growing and nurturing spirit, whose hugs I never tire of receiving and a smile the lights up any room. I love them both. They are the best women in my life and I have the honor of being daughter & mother.

To the young men in my life, my sons Cash & Cobra. My young men are each so unique; Cobra inspires me to be creative and take it easy every once in a while; Cash inspires me to be driven while reminding me to stay the course in the face of adversity. I love you both.

To my Husband John, my rock, my last date, love of my life and man of my dream; he is my everything. Thank you for believing in me and listening to the fleeting moments of insecurities and keeping me on track. I love you Honey Bunny.

Ginger Rockey-Johnson

Contents

PREFACE 17

INTRODUCTION 21

KNOW WHO YOU ARE 27

ARCHETYPES EXPLAINED 28
BRAND ARCHETYPE #1: THE SAGE 29
BRAND ARCHETYPE #2: THE INNOCENT 30
BRAND ARCHETYPE #3: THE EXPLORER..31
BRAND ARCHETYPE #4: THE RULER 32
BRAND ARCHETYPE #5: THE CREATOR 33
BRAND ARCHETYPE #6: THE CAREGIVER 34
BRAND ARCHETYPE #7: THE MAGICIAN 35
BRAND ARCHETYPE #8: THE HERO..36
BRAND ARCHETYPE #9: THE OUTLAW 37
BRAND ARCHETYPE #10: THE LOVER..38
BRAND ARCHETYPE #11: THE JESTER...39
BRAND ARCHETYPE #12: THE REGULAR GUY/GIRL..................40
TANGIBLE BUSINESS GOALS 42
LOGO & GRAPHIC DESIGN 43

KNOW WHO THEY ARE 47
YOUR COMPETITION'S MEDIA PRESENCE 49
YOUR IDEAL CLIENT, NOT THE AVERAGE ONE 51

THE INTERNET SALES FUNNEL 53
BROWSERS 55
CONSUMERS 56
PROSPECTS 60
CUSTOMERS 64
RAVING FANS 66

KNOW HOW IT WORKS **69**

KEYWORD RESEARCH, KEY PHRASES, & KEY WORD IDENTIFICATION FOR YOUR SPECIFIC MARKET 71
- IT'S SOCIAL + SEARCH 71
- KEYWORDS IS KING 72

SEARCH ENGINES DEMYSTIFIED 75
- LOCAL SEARCHES - WHY, WHAT, HOW 77
- MOBILE MARKETING 79
- 3 TYPES OF SEARCH ENGINES 81
- META DATA – MYTH OR NEEDED? 88

ONLINE ADVERTISING & PAY PER CLICK 92

KNOW HOW THE BASICS FIT TOGETHER AND **95**

WEBSITE DEVELOPMENT 97
- AUDIENCE 97
- CONTENT 97
- LANDING PAGES, MICRO-SITES, & BANNERS 99
- COMPATIBILITY AND IMAGE RESTRICTIONS 99
- CALL TO ACTION 101
- KEY ISSUES IN WEBSITE DESIGN 102

KNOW YOU CAN BE SOCIAL ONLINE **109**

SOCIAL MEDIA 111
- SOCIAL MEDIA IS A GAME CHANGER 112
- B2B USE OF SOCIAL MEDIA WILL ONLY GROW IN YEARS TO COME ... 114
- SMALL AND LARGE B2BS ARE MORE SOCIAL 114
- THE TOP 4 SOCIAL CHANNELS ARE GETTING B2B ACTION 115

E3 – THE REAL POWER OF SOCIAL MEDIA 116
ENTERTAINMENT 116
ENGAGEMENT 117
EDUCATION 118
EXPOSURE IS EVERYTHING 119
MEASUREMENT AND ANALYSIS 122

SOCIAL MEDIA OPTIMIZATION..124
COORDINATE YOUR SOCIAL CHANNELS 128
SOCIAL MEDIA CHANNELS – WHICH ONE TO CHOOSE?? 132
FACEBOOK 134
GOOGLE + ...140
TWITTER..143
LINKEDIN 150
PINTEREST 155
INSTAGRAM 158
GRAPHICS & DIMENSIONS:..161
- FACEBOOK 162
- TWITTER 162
- LINKEDIN 162
- GOOGLE+ 162
- PINTEREST 162
- YOUTUBE 162

WHEN & HOW OFTEN TO POST TO SOCIAL MEDIA 163
FLIRTING WITH THE FINE ART OF FREQUENCY 164
KNOW WHERE TO POST 168
SOCIAL MEDIA MANAGEMENT TOOLS – SIMPLICITY FOR YOU 169
DEMOGRAPHICS AND YOUR AUDIENCE..185
12 SOCIAL MEDIA MISTAKES COMPANIES MAKE..................................187

KNOW CONTENT & STRATEGIES WORK......................192

CONTENT STRATEGIES – WHERE TO FIND MORE WHEN I HAVE NONE! 194
RSS & BLOGS 194
PRESS RELEASES, ARTICLE WRITING, & SYNDICATION 195

PROMOTIONS, DAILY DEALS & COUPONS 199

SOCIAL REVIEWS 200

SUMMARY 202

Preface

It is from my past pains in life, that I am driven to help others succeed, to never give up, to never give in. That is being remarkable…using your life's pain to push you and motivate you to help others. My drive in life is truly internal and deeply rooted. For some, it's not, and I get that, but for me, it's a life worth living, and those moments I call soulful times, are the ones that make it amazing. My life is my drive to succeed, to excel, to compete…with myself, to be the best me I can possibly be, and to take as many others with me on this journey as possible. I may be beaten up and beaten down in my choice in life, just like you… I just will never quit, never stop. I can't. It would mean that I disappointed someone and didn't fulfill what I meant to do in life.

My passion to help others in whatever I do comes from the same source. It is important to me to help others not be invisible and not feel that if they disappeared tomorrow, no one would notice. I wrote this book for that same reason. Marketing is all about not being invisible.

You're Not Invisible, Don't Let Your Brand Be Either is a book dedicated to helping you understand how to create a visible brand. It matters, because you matter. I believe that you are here to serve customers who are in alignment with you and your business. They need you and your business. That is the drive, the reason why, the motivation to get up in the morning, to search for new ways to make your product or service better, faster, and easier. This is my "why," and I am delighted to help you find yours!

My hopes are that this book serves as a guide to demystifying marketing, empowering you, and giving you a level of comfort that you can do it, or at the very least be an informed decision maker without feeling like you have been bamboozled.

Marketing online is more than just a suggested path for achieving and fulfilling sales or reaching a broader audience. In today's business and beyond, it is a necessity!

This book is also the first step of three in the journey. Understanding the confusion and then How to Be Remarkable…How To Stand Out.

Blessings and Peace,

Ginger Rockey-Johnson,

The *Original* Spice Girl of Tampa Bay

If you so choose, every mistake can lead to greater understanding and effectiveness. If you so choose, every frustration can help you to be more patient and more persistent

Ralph Marston

Introduction

Let me say, I am not the best technician, but ideas I can come up with all day long. Out of the Box, unprecedented and completely on brand. It takes my awesome team to execute it. Being remarkable at who you are and what you do has very little to do with getting it technically correct. If you are not the technical person but really want to have that *Remarkability Factor*, you have the right book in your hands. Remarkability is for those who need to understand what your team needs to execute. It is for the entrepreneur who is just starting out and the business owner who just can't make sense of it all. Take it one step at a time and you'll be fine. But first, you have to understand something very, very basic.

In marketing, your products and services are irrelevant, it's the emotion you're tapping into to elicit a response that say "I have to have that" from your buyer. I've said for years: People don't buy products. The product or service is completely irrelevant. They buy the person in front of them. Shoot, you could sell dog crap if you loved and believed in it and that confidence would be felt by your audience and they would buy. Don't accept that? Watch any dance show, modeling show or reality TV show and those who are technically the best aren't the ones who win. It is the ones whose confidence is greatest and that confidence is felt in the audience.

The people who get hired at the best jobs, get the guy or girl, aren't the ones who went through the checklist and did it by the book. It's the people who are liked the most. It's the people who are good at being unique, standing out… who are remarkable in society. People buy you for who you are, not the neighbor you think you need to be or the TV star that you think has it better. People buy the unique, the odd, the stand out. They look for who you are, and what you stand for, all from the first encounter with you.

Now I know that you aren't buying that just yet or you may be saying "Yeah, I know, I know, BUT I don't know how to do the technically correct stuff either and I don't want to look silly or ruin my brand doing it wrong. I just want to get that down first." No worries. I have been using this entire content with nearly every client and hundreds of small businesses for nearly a decade. Do the right things the first time; they are not hard. It just takes time to learn.

After that, and most importantly, be yourself and be the best version of You. If you want to have multi-colored hair today and purple tomorrow…DO IT! I do! When it comes to being the best that is me, I push myself hard, every day. I am driven to get things done and take a step forward every day. I am the best at being me and I love it. I can honestly say that I love being me and I have zero desire to be someone else, just me. You are the only reason you are not exponentially more relevant, more dynamic, and more remarkable than you are right now. That is what being remarkable is, be the best you version of you and then PUSH the boundaries.

An online marketing plan is more than just a suggested path for achieving and fulfilling sales and reaching a broader audience, in 2015 & beyond it's a necessity. It's been a necessity for a few years, but if you are just getting started have no fear. If you have a business now, you'll inevitably hear these questions, "What's your website address?", "Can I have your business card?", "Are you on social media?"

A plan isn't complicated, it's a simple outline with all the questions answered that people will or could ask you. You'll also find along the way, that you'll have questions that you'll want to put in writing as well. This is a necessary step just like having a plan for vacation. The more your personality demands of your plan, the more you will write it out, e.g., where you want to go, places you want to visit, things you want to buy to take home to friends and family, etc. You even plan for how much money you want to start saving for your upcoming vacation so you don't run short. This is the same thing, it's just that not everything in life is as enjoyable as saving for the annual vacation.

As a business owner you might even be skeptical that you can even take a vacation or you haven't taken one is many years. Your marketing plan must outline the necessary changes to implement or improve each of these areas so that rest becomes a reality and not the dream.

For your note taking pleasure I have given you plenty of writing space throughout this book. ***Use it. Write in it.*** I designed it for you to be able to be keep everything you need in one place and the same size as your iPad mini, so no excuses. Don't bother with that notebook that you are not going to be able to keep up with, get lost, or not read your scribbling later. Just write throughout this book and have it all in one place. In my next book, we'll be building on your remarkability.

Let's get started.

Presence

Know Who You Are

Know Who You Are

Knowing who you are as a brand is the starting point. Now this is not the same as who you are as a person, although it could be. It is most likely something else. Start with understanding your brand's personality, your archetype.

In the next section, we'll go into what an Archetype is. Archetypes help you maintain a brand personality. Once you have identified your brand style or, if you don't have that brand personality, help you develop your marketing and business around it. It would be like a Christian saying that we want to be Christ-like and spend a lifetime attempting to learn and grow into that.

Spend time identifying your brands Archetype from the definitions listed In the next section. If you are stuck between a two types, mark the pages. Come back to it a few days later and decide which you would like.

Once you have it, make sure that it is known to all of your employees and vendors. Make sure that all of your company's Mission & Vision convey that to all who experience your company. Embed it in the very core of who you are as a brand and don't deviate from your personality as your company grows.

Archetypes Explained

The term "archetype" was first used by the psychologist, Carl Gustav Jung. He referenced and used the concept of archetype in his theory of the human psyche. He believed that archetypes, reside within the collective unconscious of people the world over. He believed that Archetypes represent the fundamentals of human ideas and experiences as humanity evolved and without doubt, how they express deep emotions.

Although there are many different archetypes, I prefer the twelve that Jung defined as primary types that symbolize basic human motivations. Each type has its own set of values, meanings and personality traits. Also, the twelve types are divided into three sets of four, namely Ego, Soul and Self. The types in each set share a common driving source, for example types within the Ego set are driven to fulfill ego-defined agendas.

Most people, if not all, have several archetypes at play in their personality construct; however, one archetype tends to dominate the personality in general. It can be helpful to know which archetypes are at play in oneself and others, especially loved ones, friends and co-workers, in order to gain personal insight into behaviors and motivations.

There are several articles on the Internet about Archetypes, I like the explanations and examples that give you something you can relate to and understand it.

Brand Archetype #1: The Sage

Quote: "The sage wears clothes of coarse cloth but carries jewels in his bosom; He knows himself but does not display himself; He loves himself but does not hold himself in high esteem." ~ Lao Tzu

Motto: The truth will set you free.
Driving desire: to find truth
Goal: to use intelligence and analysis to understand the world
Biggest fear: being duped, misled—or ignorance.
Strategy: seeking out information and knowledge; self-reflection and understanding thought processes
Weakness: can study details forever and never act
Talent: wisdom, intelligence

Also known as: expert, scholar, detective, advisor, thinker, philosopher, academic, researcher, thinker, planner, professional, mentor, teacher, contemplative, guru

Sage archetypes in the wild:

- provide expertise or information to customers
- encourage customers to think
- based on new scientific findings or esoteric knowledge
- supported by research-based facts
- differentiate from others whose quality or performance is suspect

Archetype examples: BBC, CNN, Gallup, PBS

Brand Archetype #2: The Innocent

Quote: "Innocence is always unsuspicious." ~ Joseph Joubert

Motto: We are young and free.
Driving desire: to get to paradise
Goal: to be happy
Greatest fear: to be punished for doing something bad or wrong
Strategy: to do things right
Weakness: boring for all their naive innocence
Talent: faith and optimism

Also known as: utopian, traditionalist, naive, mystic, saint, romantic, dreamer

Innocent archetypes in the wild:

- offer a simple solution to a problem
- associate with goodness, morality, simplicity, nostalgia or childhood
- low or moderate pricing
- companies with straightforward values
- differentiate from brands with poor reputations

Archetype examples: Dove soap, Ben & Jerry's ice cream

Brand Archetype #3: The Explorer

Quote: "Exploration is really the essence of the human spirit." ~ Frank Borman

Motto: Don't fence me in.
Driving desire: the freedom to find out who you are through exploring the world
Goal: to experience a better, more authentic, more fulfilling life
Biggest fear: getting trapped, conformity, and inner emptiness
Strategy: journey, seeking out and experiencing new things, escape from boredom
Weakness: aimless wandering, becoming a misfit
Talent: autonomy, ambition, being true to one's soul

Also known as: seeker, iconoclast, wanderer, individualist, pilgrim

Explorer archetypes in the wild:

- helps people feel free, nonconformist or pioneering
- rugged and sturdy or for use in the great outdoors or in dangerous settings
- can be purchased from a catalog or on the Internet
- help people express their individuality
- can be purchased for consumption on the go
- differentiate from a successful regular guy/gal brand or conformist brand
- culture that creates new and exciting products or experiences

Archetype examples: Indiana Jones, Jeep, Marlboro

Brand Archetype #4: The Ruler

Quote: "He who is to be a good ruler must have first been ruled." ~ Aristotle

Motto: Power isn't everything, it's the only thing.
Driving desire: control
Goal: create a prosperous, successful family or community
Strategy: exercise power
Greatest fear: chaos, being overthrown
Weakness: being authoritarian, unable to delegate, out of touch with reality
Talent: responsibility, leadership

Also known as: boss, leader, aristocrat, king, queen, politician, role model, manager or administrator

Ruler archetypes in the wild:

- high-status product or service used by powerful people to enhance their power
- make people more organized
- offer a lifetime guarantee
- empower people to maintain or enhances their grip on power
- has a regulatory or protective function
- moderate to high pricing
- differentiate from populist brands or clear leaders in the field
- market leaders offering a sense of security and stability in a chaotic world

Archetype examples: IBM, Microsoft

Brand Archetype #5: The Creator

Quote: "Life isn't about finding yourself. Life is about creating yourself."
~ George Bernard Shaw

Motto: If you can imagine it, it can be done.
Driving desire: to create things of enduring value
Goal: to realize a vision
Greatest fear: mediocre vision or execution
Strategy: develop artistic control and skill
Task: to create culture, express own vision
Weakness: perfectionism, bad solutions
Talent: creativity and imagination

Also known as: artist, inventor, innovator, muse, musician, writer or dreamer

Creator archetypes in the wild:

- promote self-expression, give customers choices and options, help foster innovation or is artistic in design
- creative fields like marketing, public relations, the arts, or technological innovation
- differentiate from "do-it-all" brands that leave little room for the imagination
- "do-it-yourself and save money" approach
- customer has the time to be creative
- organization with a creative culture

Archetype examples: Lego, Sony, Crayola

Brand Archetype #6: The Caregiver

Quote: "When you're a caregiver, you need to realize that you've got to take care of yourself, because—not only are you going to have to rise to the occasion to help someone else—but you have to model for the next generation." ~ Naomi Judd

Motto: Love your neighbor as yourself.
Driving desire: to protect and care for others
Goal: to help others
Greatest fear: selfishness and ingratitude
Strategy: doing things for others
Weakness: martyrdom, being exploited
Talent: compassion, generosity

Also known as: saint, altruist, parent, helper, supporter

Caregiver archetypes in the wild:

- give customers a competitive advantage
- support families (products from fast-food to minivans) or is associated with nurturing (e.g. cookies, teaching materials)
- serve the public sector, e.g. health care, education, aid programs and other caregiving fields
- help people stay connected with and care about others
- help people care for themselves
- likely a non-profit or charitable cause

Archetype examples: Mother Teresa, Johnson's Baby Shampoo

Brand Archetype #7: The Magician

Quote: "Dream no small dream; it lacks magic. Dream large. Then make the dream real." ~ Donald Wills Douglas

Motto: I make things happen.
Driving desire: understanding the fundamental laws of the universe
Goal: to make dreams come true
Greatest fear: unintended negative consequences
Strategy: develop a vision and live by it
Weakness: becoming manipulative
Talent: finding win-win solutions, making the complex appear simple

Also known as: visionary, catalyst, inventor, charismatic leader, shaman, healer, medicine man

Magician archetypes in the wild:

- promise to transform customers
- product or service is transformative
- may have a new-age quality
- consciousness-expanding
- user-friendly or contemporary
- spiritual connotations
- medium to high pricing

Archetype examples: Disney, Dreamscape Multimedia, Oil of Olay

Brand Archetype #8: The Hero

Quote: "A hero has faced it all; he need not be undefeated, but he must be undaunted." ~ Andrew Bernstein

Motto: Where there's a will, there's a way.
Driving desire: to prove one's worth through courageous acts
Goal: expert mastery in a way that improves the world
Greatest fear: weakness, vulnerability, being a "chicken"
Strategy: to be as strong and competent as possible
Weakness: arrogance, always needing another battle to fight
Talent: competence and courage

Also known as: warrior, crusader, rescuer, superhero, savior, soldier, dragon slayer, the winner and the team player

Hero archetypes in the wild:

- inventions or innovations that will have a major impact on the world
- help people be all they can be
- solve a major social problem or encourage others to do so
- have clear opponent you want to beat
- underdog or challenger brands
- products and services that are strong and help people do tough jobs exceptionally well
- differentiate from competitors with problems following through or keeping their promises ("brand enemy" positioning)
- customers see themselves as good, moral citizens

Archetype examples: Nike, Superman

Brand Archetype #9: The Outlaw

Quote: "Love is the ultimate outlaw. It just won't adhere to any rules. The most any of us can do is sign on as its accomplice." ~ Tom Robbins

Motto: Rules are made to be broken.
Driving desire: revenge or revolution
Goal: to overturn what isn't working
Greatest fear: to be powerless or ineffectual
Strategy: disrupt, destroy, or shock
Weakness: crossing over to the dark side, crime
Talent: outrageousness, radical freedom

Also known as: rebel, revolutionary, wild man, the misfit, or iconoclast

Outlaw archetypes in the wild:

- appeal to customers or employees who feel disenfranchised from society
- help retain values that are threatened by emerging ones
- pave the way for revolutionary new attitudes
- low to moderate pricing
- break with industry conventions

Archetype examples: Harley-Davidson, Apple

Brand Archetype #10: The Lover

Quote: "A true lover always feels in debt to the one he loves." ~ Ralph W. Sockman

Motto: You're the only one.
Driving desire: intimacy and experience
Goal: being in a relationship with the people, work and surroundings they love
Greatest fear: being alone, a wallflower, unwanted, unloved
Strategy: to become more and more physically and emotionally attractive
Weakness: outward-directed desire to please others at risk of losing own identity
Talent: passion, gratitude, appreciation, and commitment

Also known as: partner, friend, intimate, enthusiast, sensualist, spouse, team-builder

Lover archetypes in the wild:

- help people belong, find friends or partners
- help people have a good time
- low to moderate pricing
- freewheeling, fun-loving organizational structure
- differentiate from self-important, overconfident brands

Archetype examples: Victoria's Secret, Lady Godiva

Brand Archetype #11: The Jester

Quote: "Cheerfulness is the best promoter of health and is as friendly to the mind as to the body." ~ Joseph Addison

Motto: You only live once.
Driving desire: to live in the moment with full enjoyment
Goal: to have a great time and lighten up the world
Greatest fear: being bored or boring others
Strategy: play, make jokes, be funny
Weakness: frivolity, wasting time
Talent: joy

Also known as: fool, trickster, joker, practical joker or comedian

Jester archetypes in the wild:

- give people a sense of belonging
- help people have a good time
- low to moderate pricing
- fun-loving companies
- differentiate from self-important, overconfident established brands

Archetype examples: Motley Fool, Muppets

Brand Archetype #12: The Regular Guy/Girl

Quote: "I understand the common man because I understand me in that regard, at least." ~ Vince McMahon

Motto: All men and women are created equal.
Driving desire: connecting with others
Goal: to belong
Greatest fear: to be left out or to stand out from the crowd
Strategy: develop ordinary solid virtues, be down to earth, the common touch
Weakness: losing one's own self in an effort to blend in or for the sake of superficial relationships
Talent: realism, empathy, lack of pretense

Also known as: good old boy, everyman, the person next door, the realist, the working stiff, the solid citizen, the good neighbor, the silent majority

Regular Guy or Girl archetypes in the wild:

- giving people a sense of belonging
- offers everyday functionality
- low to moderate pricing
- solid companies with a down-home organizational culture
- differentiate from elitist or higher-priced brands

Archetype examples: Home Depot, Wendy's

So what does all of this have to do with knowing who you are? When you with someone in person, you can get to know them, read their body language, and hear the inflections in their voice. You can get to know them and make your own decision about who they are and if they are someone you want to be friends with. Brands need the same thing. Review the brand archetypes and decide who you are as a brand and develop all your language, actions, tone, and brand voice around your chosen archetype. When maintained consistently, your fans and customers will come to know what to expect.

<u>Plan of Action</u>: Spend some time defining who you are as a brand and stick with it. Include your archetype in your corporate identity documents and share it with your team.

Tangible Business Goals

In your marketing efforts it is critical to stay focused on what the goal for each channel is. That is to say, what EXACTLY do you want to accomplish and how do you know when you have "arrived"? A channel is simply a method used to promote your business. For example, Facebook is one channel and it has a specific purpose and strategy that works best for marketing purposes. Twitter has a different purpose and strategy. We'll get into the marketing channels a bit later. For now, you must decide why you want to market your business.

- Build awareness
- Strengthen relationships with clients, prospects, and influencers
- Better understand your buyers
- Improve customer service
- Identify new product ideas
- Increase web site traffic
- Improve search engine rankings
- Drive traffic to your trade show displays at events
- Generate leads

Deliver to your audience what they are looking for, e.g., Pictures & Videos! Displaying your craft and what your talent is capable of delivering will farther than any print ad alone. You need to develop a strategy that shows them what they are missing and creates desire for a luxury item they didn't know they needed.

Logo & Graphic Design

People are visual creatures. We recognize and search for symbols. You need a logo design that's visually appealing and speaks to the audience as well as your brand. You can see the impact a logo has on brand recognition with McDonalds' golden arches or Home Depot's construction symbol.

Let me give you a different example… There are many direct sales companies out there and many representatives of those companies. Those companies maintain its branding consistency by dictating how their imagery (logo) is used. If the representative must order business cards from that company, they all look the same. The imagery is consistent. So as an independent representative to Stand Out? It is NOT dependent upon the stuff. It's dependent up on the person, but consistency to the consumer is maintained in the imagery.

<u>Plan of Action:</u> Create a logo that makes you memorable, represents you, and conveys a message. Create logo and branded print materials that send the same cohesive message and includes purposeful consideration to colors, font and font style. Most importantly, make sure your logo and messaging is consistent with your Archetype.

Competitive Differentiators And Unique Selling Proposition (USP)

It's not enough to have a business and say "we provide excellent" customer service." If I asked your competition, would they say the same thing? Odds are that they think they deliver great customer service as well. You need MORE than that. You need to stand out in every instance of business, including analyzing how to stand out above your competition.

In the next section I've included two tables to give you an idea of what you need, at a minimum, to evaluate, along with some of the standards that are present in any good competitive analysis. This is tough for many new business owners, so take your time and focus. It's better to do it once and do it well, than to rush through it "to get it done" and have to repeat it because it doesn't reflect enough information for you to make business decisions.

Competition

&

Audience

Know Who They Are

Your Competition's Media Presence

List out your competitors. Check out your competitors' social media profiles and what they are doing with them. In this table, are the most popular social media and Internet presence websites, but be sure to also capture other Internet properties that are important to your business and industry. It is important to add elements to your table if they exist in your competitors so you can properly determine IF it is a critical element or just irrelevant. Don't guess, document, document, document.

Competitor Name	eCommerce Site / Website	Facebook	Twitter	Pinterest	Instagram	YouTube	Foursquare	Google+
Your Business								

You need to analyze at least 3 other businesses and up to 7. Don't go overboard and get tied into analysis-paralysis.

Your Competition's Business

<u>List out your competitors</u>. Check out your competitors' business model. While there could be many more elements you need to evaluate for your business needs, here are some basic elements to make sure to capture.

Use an excel spreadsheet to capture your information and save it with your corporate documents so you can review it periodically to stay in line with your brand focus.

Competitor Name	Product / Service	Price per Unit	Quality	Customer Service	Distribution	Location	Demographics focused
Your Business							

Now that you can clearly see your competition, it's time to focus on your business and your potential customer base.

Your Ideal Client, Not the Average One

Knowing who your audience is, is the first step in knowing who your buyers are and understanding where they spend their time online. It is not as easy as saying "I'm a Chiropractor and I can help anyone with a spine." or the skin care specialist who says that their customer is "…anyone with skin…", I'm calling you on that one right now.

If that were true, if it were true that anyone was your client, you'll be a flat broke business serving many amazing charities in our community. It's just a lie that you tell yourself so others will think better of you and you hope they will have compassion and do business with you. We all know its B.S. and worse yet, we now know you are flat broke begging for anyone to give you money. Is that what you want? Pity Business?

Get Real. You want customers who can pay you, who make a certain income. Identify the ideal client or customer first. When you are making what you want to make, you'll have time to help those you want to help. You cannot help others until you can help yourself. There is a reason the airlines tell you put on your oxygen mask first before helping others.

Get clear about who your audience is. Here are some questions to help you get clear about who your target audience is before you start creating further.

1) My average customer is…
2) Who are they? (Are YOU one of them? Are your friends one of them?):

3) Are you currently focusing on your IDEAL audience or are you focusing on people you have access to?:

4) Likes / Dislikes (What do they value?):

5) What do they want from you? (What are their underlying goals? or What expectations do they have of you?):

6) WHY are they motivated to buy? (Are they motivated?):

7) My IDEAL customer is…:
   a. Gender:
   b. Age:
   c. Income:
   d. Home Life:
   e. Work Life:
   f. Geography:

The Internet Sales Funnel

Know your sales cycle. If your customers have a long lead time – meaning that from the time you first get to know them until the time they buy from you is X days, you must know what that cycle is, so that you don't get discouraged along the way. Right now, if you have no idea what that cycle is, you may be experiencing frustration, concern, and panic that you aren't going to make your business successful. When in reality, you might just be in the middle of your sales cycle.

It is entirely unrealistic to expect someone to buy the moment they meet you. Can it happen? Sure, but it's an unrealistic expectation. So know how long in days, as well as the number of "contacts" or "touches" it takes to convert a prospect to a customer.

In the previous section you should have clearly defined WHO your ideal customer is. There is no sense in taking on customer's who cannot benefit from your experience or who are not a good fit for you. It will leave you with less joy in your day and exhausted. These are the things that you need to take into consideration when developing your brand. Attracting an audience is not good enough; it's all about attracting the RIGHT audience that you can deliver remarkable results to and _Stand Out_ in your field!

The sales funnel starts with developing "collateral" that attracts your ideal customer. **Collateral** means anything that you publish, print, show to your prospect that clearly conveys, "Here's what I do and what I can do for you". From your print: brochures, flyers, business cards, print ads, gift away items, checklists, etc., to your online presence: website, email signature, profile photos… everything. So let's take it from the top shall we?

Browsers > Consumers > Prospects > Customers > Raving Fans

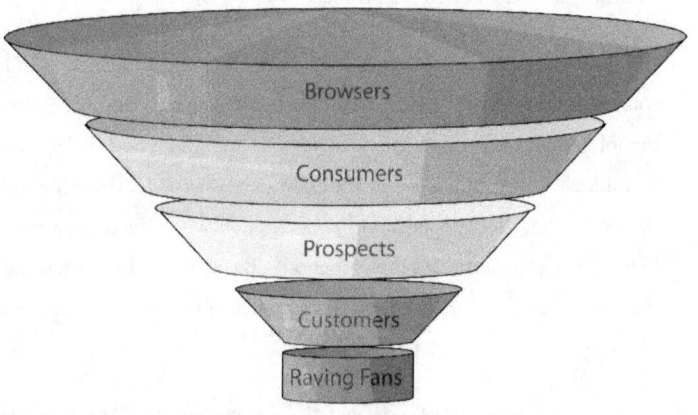

Browsers

Browsers are people who are aware that other options to what they need exist, but they are often unaware that your company, brand, product or service can help them. They are searching for their symptoms (for the solutions), the topics related (to those their friends have said were related), similar products or services to those that come up either in conversation or when they search online, etc., but they are not 100% certain about where they want to spend their money. They are surfing, researching, and narrowing their interests.

If your business's marketing strategy were to include reaching this audience as a part of your sales process, understand that the money and time spent would result in only brand recognition. While you would gain valuable traffic from the frequent new visitors investigating their options, the ROI is very low. People want to do their due diligence before making purchasing decisions.

Brands with a disposable income for their ad budget usually invest their dollars here. This strategy is used not for a return on investment for dollars spent in the sense of traffic in the door, but in the buzz it creates in the minds of the consumers. The imagery flashes in the consumers mind when a purchasing decision needs to be made and the brand appears to be "everywhere" so therefore, it must have what I need.

Consumers

Consumers are defined in this funnel as those who are "consuming your content." They are feeding themselves with your content to see if it satisfies them, similar to eating a meal. You are hungry, but you are unsure of what you want. When consumers first engage here, they aren't sure that you will satisfy them either. If you do, they keep eating. Consumers are willing to exchange their valuable information for great content, but you have to give them something without asking them for anything, in order to show them that you have great content. There are several strategies that work in converting browsers or "looky-loos" into consumers but it starts with one word....FREE.

Everyone loves to get something for free. Free information is info that, if you did a search yourself, you could find the answers as well. Just be yourself, and deliver your opinion. This can be in several forms; just give away the low hanging fruit. Here's some content that performs really well.

Infographics – a visual image such as a chart or diagram used to represent information or data. "A good Infographic is worth a thousand words". You've seen these all over any social media site, newspaper, store window, flyers, and brochures. Here is one of mine just to give you an example, but there are literally limitless possibilities to creating an Infographic. Just search Google for "Infographics" and go to the images tab and you'll see tons of examples.

There are some free and not so free tools you can use online to creating an Infographic. Here are just a few, each do different types of Infographics depending on what you'd like to achieve. Then there is always hiring

designers to craft your custom images as well.

   a) Visualize.me
   b) Easel.ly
   c) Piktochart.com
   d) Infogr.am
   e) Visual.ly
   f) Vennage.com
   g) Dipity.com

<u>Step-by-step instructions</u> – Everyone wants to be an expert. DIY is the latest trend in online solutions. Information is available everywhere from blogs to YouTube. Giving your audience the experience and expertise they desire will go a long way to converting your consumers to prospects.

<u>Video tutorials</u> – Lights camera action! Today's audience is all about the video content. Not everyone is into video, so pay special attention to how your target audience wants to be reached. But no matter what, you need to be vlogging. Video Blogging is an easy way to create content and repurpose it for multiple uses. Give all your information away. Trust me, the information is out there anyway so you might as well capitalize on the audience who is searching for it. There are the people out there who are only interested in the information and not good customers for you anyway.

<u>Blog posts</u> – Share your opinions, bold and radical statements on your own blog and draw more of a following to your point of view. You don't have to a great eloquent writer, just an honest one. Share great articles you see in newsletters you receive, read online or other sources and add your opinion to the article for your readers, just make sure to give proper credit to the source. It's a great way to give and get recognition by sharing someone else's content. You need more than 300 words to be able to rank in search engine and over 500 words you'll be too wordy for today's busy person. So keep it short and sweet. If you feel a great writing day come on, write in a document and split it up into a few blogs. Scheduling these to post in advance saves time and frustration when life gets busy.

The secret to a good blog is in this recipe:

a) 300 – 500 words
b) Consistent content style (be yourself)
c) Delivery is consistent (weekly, every 2 weeks, or monthly at the least)
d) Add an image
e) Schedule at least 6 blogs in advance and get into a habit of adding two blogs at a time.

Checklists – Give your audience the To-Do List that they want! In general, people do well when you tell them what they need to do in list form. The information is digestible and less frustrating when all they have to do is follow a checklist.

Podcasts – Podcasts are simple recordings of you explaining, talking, interviewing, or clowning around. They are pure audio that can be added to their iTunes and listened to on the road.

Prospects

When Consumers have viewed all of the information that they are interested in within their reach, you give them more… in exchange for their information. Now don't get greedy, just their email and their name.

If you ask for too much info on the first contact, you are likely to get bogus information just to populate the field. This is converting a consumer of your free information into a real prospect. Have this directly populate into your email marketing campaigns list. It's a time saving tip that many people forget but it will keep you compliant with the email spamming rules and save you a frustrating time with added typos. Make sure the list is named something that is easy to understand when you review it later. I call mine "Freebies First." I know. It's too simple, right? Fortunately, though, it doesn't need to be complicated.

This list name tells me that they consumed as much free information they wanted and are ready to reach just beyond their grasp. It also tells me that they are most likely going to stay in my sales funnel for a while.

When a browser lands on your site from investigative research, they may subscribe to your content just to keep you in mind. So don't expect everyone in your newly created list to be good consumers. Meaning there are three categories of people who complete this step.

1) The people who are interested, on some level, to what you have to say but are not seriously paying attention. They just wanted the one piece of information that you offered and may promptly unsubscribe at the next follow up point (whether it's your next email, or if you call them, etc.). The trick with this group is to be

very engaging and helpful at the next point of contact or you risk losing them. They could very well be your target audience but may have been spammed one too many times and you are the one that they are hoping is different. It is essential to speak your audience's language to help you attract and relate to your ideal customer. This is one of the first points of contact with reaching those who are your target market. If you have attempted to capture "everyone is my market" all you'll end up doing is annoying some people (those who are not your target) or turning off those who are your target market because they don't think you understand them well enough. You may find a few customers here and here but odds are that you will be left with the dismal few who are desperate to find someone to help them and that might be you.

2) The consumers who use the 'newsletter' or junk email address. Come on we all have them. The email that we all use to sign up for stuff but rarely check it or open it to "Mark All As Read" or delete all the email in the inbox.

3) The people who have a real problem, in your target audience, that are considering you to have the solution that fits their needs. Speak their language and deliver what you KNOW that your target market needs and it opens the door to a conversion.

Fast Fact! The Rule of 10: *Everything in life works in a statistical rule of 10. If you want 1 new Customer, you need to have 10 new Prospects. In order to have 10 new Prospects, you need to have 100 new Customers, to reach 100 new Customers; you need to be in front of 1,000 Browsers.*

Raving Fans help reduce your Rule of 10, and we'll get into that one later. Social Media is critical to reaching new Browsers with the least amount of out-of-pocket expense.

This is about helping prospects understand that you have the solution to their problem. Not all content to your prospects has to be free; some can be given away as loss leaders to drive traffic to you. If your average price point is $500, you might consider have a prospecting offer that is $99 or $200. Something that is significantly less in content and offer than you would deliver but still contains value to your audience.

Specific website pages do this. Your "About Us" and "Services" pages can educate prospects about your services. Useful, authoritative blog posts get them engaged with your brand. The type of content you want to create will educate the prospects about their problems and the solutions that your organization offers. Here is some content that performs very well:

1) How-to's – this is more in depth than the checklists you used to attract your target market. This is meant to give them the procedure. For example, on my site, I give a checklist called "14 day step by step Calendar for Social Media Success". It is free. The crafting of great content for the social media calendar and the management tools that can be used to save time while managing your social media success is a How To Guide that is subscribed to.
2) White Papers (Reports that are 5 – 10 pages in length with charts possibly showing before and after)
3) Secrets Insider Trade Information – Slideshare is a great tool to use to deliver trade secrets and have it go viral to the masses who view it on LinkedIn. Great content in numerical form will always be viewed before anything else is.

4) Extended Audio Training – This can be a password-protected area of your site that allows them access to your series of content on your expert training. It may be very basic to you but is it what your audience may need.

Customers

Congratulations! You have a new customer. Don't pat yourself on the back just yet, though. Getting new customers is like getting a new fan on Facebook; they are easy to get, harder to keep satisfied. While most businesses believe that it is a win when someone "likes" your fan page, the work has really just begun. Holding your audience's attention long enough for them to get to know you better is the toughest thing to do. So, once you have a customer, your media presence needs to step up and change direction. Have them fan you on Facebook. As a fan on your social media site, your education process should excel. Do you have them on that super-secret club group versus a page for receiving specials that only your clients can receive? Make sure you have permission to send them client only information in your email campaign? You'll create more intrigue when you tell them that this information is for clients only and it will create a buzz as clients can't help but share their new industry secrets with their friends and colleagues.

Now before you panic about them sharing your insider info with their family, remember that the more you are talked about and shared, the more viral your content becomes. There is no greater reward on many levels for the content shares, likes, backlinks to your site, and more word of mouth marketing that is free. This reduces your Rule of 10 increasing the touches it takes to get the next ideal customer.

I have seen time and time again that a business owner's biggest mistake is to treat a customer the same as a prospect and be disappointed when the turnover rate in their business is fairly low. If you have a disposable business model, then perhaps your measurement of success is not to see them come back. The kinds of businesses that this model would apply to could be a surgeon. You'd hope that the first time you saw and treated the person would be the last!

My business model is based on being disposable. We do have clients who choose to stay with us, and some have been with us for over a decade, but it is not our original model. We grow, educate, and graduate. That is our model. Grow the business; educate the owners and staff; graduate them when they are comfortable enough. So know your business model, your sales cycle, and your sales funnel to keep the wheels of income turning.

Raving Fans

Keeping a customer is actually very simple to outline, but somehow tougher to execute. Our egos get in the way, or we take it all personally. Creating raving fans is all about doing what you said you would do and when you said you would. We all have a tough time with this one and at some point we are likely to miss the mark at least once. It's okay. It's how we get up, face the music and move on that counts. Communication is the best weapon you have to keeping your customers happy and informed. If you are not the best at communicating with customers, hire someone who is. The recipe for success here is very simple:

- Do what you say you'll do.
- Keep educating your clients, so that you can share the ownership.
- Be consistent, and deliver.
- Provide the quality you'd expect to receive.
- When you screw up, acknowledge it, and own up to it.
- Fix your mistakes.
- Go the extra mile

So, beyond the obvious advice of going the extra mile to deliver exceptional service, what is the one-thread of consistency? It is truth, honesty, integrity, and communication.

<u>Plan of Action</u>

1. When you think you have been truthful enough, be more transparent.
2. When you think you have been honest with yourself, ask if you could have done more.
3. When you think you have shared all that have in you, be more vulnerable.
4. When you think you have talked enough, call them again.

Search

Know How It Works

And

Why You Get Found

Keyword Research, Key Phrases, & Key Word Identification for your Specific Market

It's Social + Search

Social media is a part of search engine optimization. I call it Social Search. Use your keywords in your social media strategy. It's not one or the other! It's both… at the same time! Everything you do on the Internet is there to stay, so make it work!

Key Phrases, or commonly referred to as a "Key Word", are highly searched terms used by your potential customers. The most beneficial terms are those they use when they are ready to make buying decisions. For your business, find the terms that people are searching for related to your business. Focusing the website to attract the customers who are searching those terms drives traffic to your website. That traffic results in increased local searches.

Keywords Is King

Definition - What does *Keyword* mean?

A keyword, in the context of search engine optimization, is a particular word or phrase that describes the contents of a webpage. Keywords are intended to act as shortcuts that sum up an entire page. Keywords form part of a webpage's metadata and help search engines match a page with an appropriate search query.

Techopedia explains *Keyword*
(*written by Cory Jensen of Technopedia*)

The role of keywords was once very central to the function of search engines. Search engines could scan sites and, if the keywords were accurate, serve those sites up as search results. However, people began abusing the keyword metadata, in an attempt to show up higher in searches, and even to rank in completely unrelated searches. For this reason, the importance of keywords in search engine optimization has been greatly reduced. Keywords are arguably still an important factor, but they are not the only factor in SEO.

This definition was written in the context of SEO.

Think of how you search for information on the Internet. You go to a search engine, such as Google.com, and type in a phrase to search for. The search engine then displays a list of websites that are relevant to the phrase you entered. This phrase is called a "keyword," and it is the main way in which we all find information on the Internet. (Thank You Technopedia. You can check out more on their blog technopedia.com)

Your target market that is looking for information online uses certain keywords or keyword phrases when searching. Your goal is to have your website or video or article appear in the search results, so that potential customers can find your website.

This can be done by performing a little keyword research. Keyword research is the process of finding out which words people are searching for when they want products or services like yours, and then optimize your pages within your website so that it appears in the search results for those keywords.

Now, not all keywords are equal. Some keywords have as many as 2 or 3 million websites listed for them. These keywords are very competitive, and hence, it's a very difficult task to rank in the search results, especially if you're just starting out.

This is where 'long-tail' keywords come in. Long-tail keywords are nothing but keyword phrases that have a low search volume. That is, they are not searched for as often as the more competitive keywords. While this means that there are fewer numbers of prospective customers searching for them, and there is also less (and sometimes non- existent) competition in the results. If you target these keywords on your website or video or article, it will much easier for you to rank for them. If you target a lot of these keywords, they add up to give you a lot of traffic easily!

Find your keywords and use them in your social media posting. Here are two tools to help you with the basics:

1) Determine which words or phrases your best customers are typing into Google, Bing, or Yahoo FIRST.

- <http://ubersuggest.org/>

2) See how well those keywords are trending; that is, are they highly searched, or are there better phrases you can use?

- <http://www.google.com/trends/>

Phrases not single words. Find the best phrases by asking the question, "What are people searching for?"

Search Engines Demystified

What is Search Engine Optimization (SEO)? Let's get a simple understanding of SEO, before we get into some details of how all the pieces work. SEO is a long term plan. Advertising is a short term plan. SEO is not advertising. Advertising is paid positioning; SEO is organic positioning. With advertising you spend money for the results. With SEO you spend a lot of effort and time.

In the simplest terms, think of this process as being similar to kids on a playground. Everyone is running around having fun, and on the side is a teacher, searching for someone. She scans the crowd, looking at the lone child sitting on the bench, the group of popular kids having fun, the group of kids watching the popular kids and wishing they could join in, and then the rag-tag group of kids who are running around wreaking havoc on everyone else.

The process we, as humans, use to search for someone is the same. We scan groups first, and in our minds, we place a label on what they are associated with that we can recognize. Then, we place mental labels on the remaining people until we systematically rule them out in our search. Whatever is left is of interest, so we approach and let the one-on-one interaction determine the relationship's fate.

Search engines work exactly the same way. It is a systematic process, designed to exponentially speed up that mental labeling and sorting that took place in our minds before the Internet. Want to put that to the test? Go to a networking function. Walk in, and start a conversation about your services without any pre-labeling or mental-sorting of the crowd.

Search engine algorithms have improved constantly in the effort to learn how to deliver those results faster and faster. Along with that, search engines continue to reduce the noise that is caused by all the "kids running around wreaking havoc," which we call "the spammers." When you hear frustration from the people who say that their website lost positioning because of the algorithm changes, keep in mind that very few really have. They may feel a shift in rankings, similar to getting on a repositioning cruise. You get on at one port, and days later, when you get off of the ship, the scenery is entirely different. Eventually, though, you can get back on the cruise ship and go home.

Search Engine Optimization (SEO) is a strategic combination of techniques designed to raise a website's ranking in the search engines' natural listings. In other words, SEO is the process of increasing the amount of visitors to a Web site by ranking high in the search results of a search engine using special tools and the targeted keywords. The higher a Web site ranks in the results of a search, the greater the chance that that site will be visited by a user. These techniques need to be continually revised and refined as the main search engines regularly update their ranking criteria.

There are different kinds of SEO, internal, external, and hosted. Internal sometimes called On Page, means that content inside the website is optimized and every page is optimized independent of each other. When you hire someone to do SEO, be specific in asking which they focus on, it's important to do all of them but you need to know what is going to happen first. External SEO or off page, is optimizing content outside of your website. Webmasters do not need access to your site to complete this work. External SEO is sometimes referred to as Hosted SEO, but more often it is referring to the directory submissions, blog commenting and sharing of your content outside of the website.

Hosted SEO is most commonly associated with Press Releases and news stories that are hosted on someone else's site and pushes their traffic to your site.

Plan of Action: Organically optimize your site to increase brand recognition and expert authority in search engines   it's a long term project but the more you invest in organic SEO, the less you'll end up needing to spend on advertising.

Local Searches - Why, What, How

More and more people are choosing the internet as their first choice to conduct research and look for local businesses. Search engines have shifted from generic search terms to localized searches with a 5 - 25 mile radius. Go to Yahoo Local, and type in 'pizza,' along with your address and you'll have all the pizza restaurants within a ten mile radius of your address. There isn't an offline medium that offers that kind of power and convenience.

Local search engine marketing uses the same techniques as outlined above, but targeted at a specific geographic region. You will include local keywords on your website by state, city, county, or region, like the Rocky Mountains, the Pacific Northwest, or New England. PPC engines like Google actually let you select regions where your ads will appear. That way, you don't have people from Texas clicking on your ads for services only available in New York.

Targeted local searches will save you money and effort. You won't have to compete with national chains or people in other regions. You'll have lower traffic but warmer leads, as people self-qualify by their locations.

This is why in the past year, the search engines like Yahoo, MSN, and Google have spent large amounts of money to improve their search functions for local markets. All the major yellow pages are now online to capture visitors. Most will sell you a package of online features along with your offline advertising. Online advertising has a number of advantages:

- Generate highly qualified leads and sales from local customers.
- Boost local offline sales - an increasing number of people search the web for products and services they buy in an offline store.
- Low cost per lead compared to print Yellow Pages and Direct Mail.
- Links directly to your company website. This allows the customer to immediately come to your website for more information on your products and services.

Mobile Marketing

Mobile Marketing is similar to Search Engine Marketing (SEM) in that it is a search engine, however SEM works on Google, Yahoo, Bing, AOL, etc. on laptops & desktops but not on mobile devices such as iPhones, iPads, Android, and other Smartphone devices. Mobile Marketing became a necessary piece of the puzzle as more than 84% of searches conducted in 2013 and more than 96% of searches conducted as of October 2014 were completed on mobile devices. In the future, the number of searches conducted via a Smartphone or mobile device is not only expected to rise to more than 95% but mobile is projected to be the primary device of the future. Now, I didn't say the ONLY device, just a primary one for the everyday user. So being in the right place and at the time your audience is searching for your services will give your business the boost ahead of the competition.

Your potential customer could have just been searching for your service in terms that are common to them. It's finding that added and creative way to use what you have to deliver to them what your next best customer needs. Displaying to them that one key nugget of information that you have to give them that one ah-ha moment while they are conducting a search. That is where you want to be. They are ready to make that buying decision, they are just looking for the business to give their money to. If they conduct that search on their mobile device, you must be there too!

Mobile Marketing will be one, if not the most important online marketing effort you do to gain ground in the fast moving world of savvy consumers & marketers.

Plan of Action: Website must be a compatible with all browsers, as well as made mobile ready for Android, iPhone, and other smartphones. If you are on WordPress, I've given you a list of the most up to date plugins to help you. Check out my website at

www.SpiceGirlofTampaBay.com/Book-Gifts

Password: AbundantBlessing

3 Types of Search Engines

Spiders

No, not the creepy crawly kind. The main or desktop search engine sends out a 'spider' or 'robot' that records all the text on your website. That text is then indexed in a database, categorized by keyword, and given a relevancy ranking. A higher relevancy ranking makes your pages appear higher when the search engine returns results to a visitor.

Main Engines – Google, Yahoo, and Bing (joint venture with Facebook, so searches in Facebook reveal Bing rankings). AOL is working on joint ventures with Yahoo in the US; however, their combined search power already impacts the remaining world.

Benefits – The Big Three, Google, Bing, AOL cover 95% of all search engine traffic. Concentrate your efforts here, and forget about the little guys.

Directories

Directories have websites submitted to them for review. The best directories are reviewed by hand and disallow affiliate sites or sites with little or no content. Most directories get very little traffic, but since the included websites are reviewed for quality, the Big Three consider them a good source to find new websites. Getting listed in directories is the most common way to build link popularity.

<u>Main Directories</u> – Business.com, DMOZ.org, GoGuides.com, JoeAnt.com, Gimpsy.org

Benefits – While these engines don't get a lot of traffic, other search engines use their results. Spider engines like Google consider directories to have high-quality content and often index the directory's additions.

Google Voice Search Changes

As 2014 comes to a close, marketers are realizing that Google's new changes address the way consumers search for information. Voice and localized search have a serious impact on the way content should be presented on sites. In 2014, marketers will need to consider the questions their customers are likely to ask of a search engines and then deliver content that answers those questions.

Businesses will also realize the importance of having basic information out there for customers to easily find. If, for instance, your local flower shop moved some time ago, yet outdated location information still exists; it will become more important than ever that the old information be removed. Those same basic details are used across the Internet in search results driving your traffic to the wrong locations. Companies like LocalMoz, LocaEze, & Neustar manage multiple listings and is easier to change your data rather than one directory listing at a time.

<u>Plan of Action</u>: Submit to directories every month as part of the overall link building strategy & branding plan. Get listed in as many directories as possible that are relevant to your business. Submit in a natural rate &

add directory submission to your marketing plan. Don't attempt to use an automated service to mass update your listings all at the same time, these third party services, boasting this, put you at risk of red flags from Google. It's a long term project but the more you invest in organic SEO, the less you'll end up needing to spend on advertising.

There are variety of tools that you can use to determine your sites rankings as it compares to your competitors. Here is an example of some of the reporting features that you should be looking for.in your own reports. This is the reports that I use to analyze a website for our clients

Top 10 Ranking Requirements Score

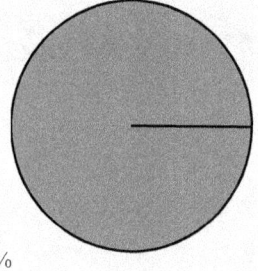

0%

The Top 10 Ranking Requirements Score of 0% means that the web page www.dgo.net meets only 0% of the requirements for a top 10 ranking on Google.com (without Places, 100 results) for the search term "custom shower doors".

Note that not all ranking factors are weighted equally, and that there are some ranking factors that cannot be taken into account because search engines do not reveal the necessary data.

Search engine ranking factors performance

Ranking Factor Importance	Factors Passed	Factors Failed
Essential (weighted most):	6	21
Very Important:	11	0
Important:	41	3
Moderately Important:	42	9
Slightly Important:	11	1
Total:	111	34

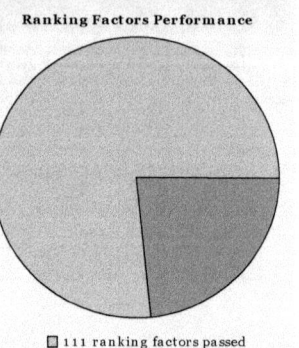

Ranking Factors Performance

- 111 ranking factors passed
- 34 ranking factors failed

Scope of this Ranking Report

5 keywords and one URL have been checked on 7 search engines. The first 10 results of each search engine have been checked.

Visibility Statistics

This table lists the found rankings for all analyzed search terms, URLs and search engines.

Listings in the first position	13
Listings in the top 5 positions	23
Listings in the top 10 positions	23
Total listings	**23**

Top 10 Listings

The left chart shows the number of top 10 rankings for your search terms, and the right chart shows the number of top 10 rankings in the search engines.

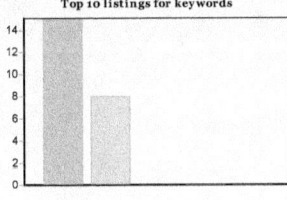
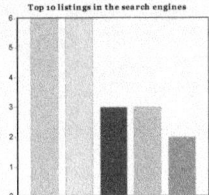

- 15 top 10 listings for "dgmirror.net"
- 8 top 10 listings for "dgmirror"
- 0 top 10 listings for "Home"
- 0 top 10 listings for "Business"
- 0 top 10 listings for "custom shower door"

Checked URLs

This table lists all URLs that have been considered for this report.

URL	Listings On Page 1
http://www.dgo.net	23
Total	**23**

Checked Keywords

This table lists all search terms for which rankings have been found in the top 10 results.

Keyword	Listings On Page 1
Business	0
custom Front door	0
Dgo	8
dgo.net	15
Home	0
Total	**23**

www.dgo.net/Mirrors.html

Search Engine	Keyword	Pos.	Page
Bing.com	dgo	3	1
Google.com	dgo.net	4	1
Google.com (100 results)	dgo.net	4	1
Yahoo.com	dgo	3	1

Ranking Results
www.dgo.net

Search Engine	Keyword	Pos.	Page
AOL.com	Business	-	-
AOL.com	custom shower door	-	-
Bing.com	dgo.net	1	1
Bing.com	Home	-	-
Google.com	Business	-	-
Google.com	custom shower door	-	-
Google.com (100 results)	dgo.net	1	1
Google.com (100 results)	Home	-	-
Google.com (without Places)	Business	-	-
Google.com (without Places)	custom shower door	-	-
Google.com (without Places, 100 results)	dgo	1	1
Google.com (without Places, 100 results)	dgo.net	1	1
Yahoo.com	dgo.net	1	1
Yahoo.com	Home	-	-

Meta Data – Myth or Needed?

Metatags Creation for the Homepage & Sub Pages – Every page is a landing page. The opinions on this is varied. This is mine. If it wasn't important, it's wouldn't be talked about at all and if it is not used then there is no harm in completing it but since it is important, then you are ahead of the mass of people who follow another opinion.

The meta description is the little blurb that describes the content of the page listed in the search results. The meta description is only visible in the SERPs (and to users who view the source code of your pages), and the description cuts off after around 155 to 170 characters.

While the meta description tag doesn't need to be optimized for search engines, it is nonetheless extremely valuable in that, to searchers, it acts as your page's ad copy. Therefore, it's important to ensure that each of your pages has a unique meta description so that users can differentiate one page from the next in search results. Targeting the same keywords over and over again in multiple meta descriptions can result in keyword cannibalization and will confuse searchers as to which of your pages is most relevant to their search.

Again, the purpose of the meta description is to compel the searcher to click on your result in the SERPs; in this sense, it is foolhardy to stuff keywords into your description tag because to a user the description of your page will look spammy. During the development phase with your website, we ensure that your meta information is useful and relevant to the site and aids in your marketing goals and does not negatively impact them.

Test your keywords.

The final way to score a site's SEO is to find out how it is doing in queries. First, in order to gain the best results possible, make sure you sign out of Google. Perform searches on targeted long-tail keywords. There are services that provide up-to-the-minute Google rank results for any site. Since I'm giving you the free method, however, we're doing it the old-fashioned way. Just Google it, and count.

SERP is Search Engine Ranking Position and is determined by several factors. The lower the position number means what position your listing has on Google's search engine. Positions 1 through 10 hold the first ten placements on Page 1 of a search engine and then it doesn't really matter. Rarely does anyone continue to search for results past the first ten placements.

Google SERP Position	**SEO Strength**
1	Excellent
2	Very Good
3-4	Good
5-10	Average
Page 2	Fair
Page 3	Poor

Plan of Action: Optimize your website and your social media profiles — including your tweets, Facebook posts, and blogs— by using these keywords. This will greatly help your search engine optimization efforts.

Link Building

Most of the top search engines use link popularity in their ranking algorithms. Google uses it as one of its most important factors in ranking sites. Increasing the amount of quality inbound links, that is links that are placed on other sites and point to your website, makes your site appear more important and more relevant to the search engines, resulting in a higher Page Rank and higher positions. There are several ways of creating inbound links but a word of caution to not get tied up in subscribing to a service that you pay for links. While these services do exist, paying for links is against terms and conditions of search engines and when caught, your site will be penalized and banned. It is nearly impossible to get that removed. So, my advice, take the long road and do it right the first time.

Many webmasters have their own popular portals and trade directories to help create links. Building a series of links that point to your site is a tactical called a *link wheel*. Link wheels are created to drive popularity of websites in an organic manner. They are intentionally used to share common and related authoritative content among experts and other people interested in that topic. So use of a link wheel in your plan is essential to share your expertise amongst many other sites that can point people to your site. Search for .edu sites to gain the most authoritative links that have the best bang for the buck.

Another option is by approaching webmasters of other high ranking popular sites, and trading links with them. Some offer ONE WAY LINKING for the website. Under ONE WAY LINKING, the website is submitted in relevant category and directory having good PageRank. ONE WAY LINKING covers the following:

- Directory Submission
- Creation of Blogs and submitting in relevant blog websites
- Responding to forum and discussion boards that are relevant to your topic.

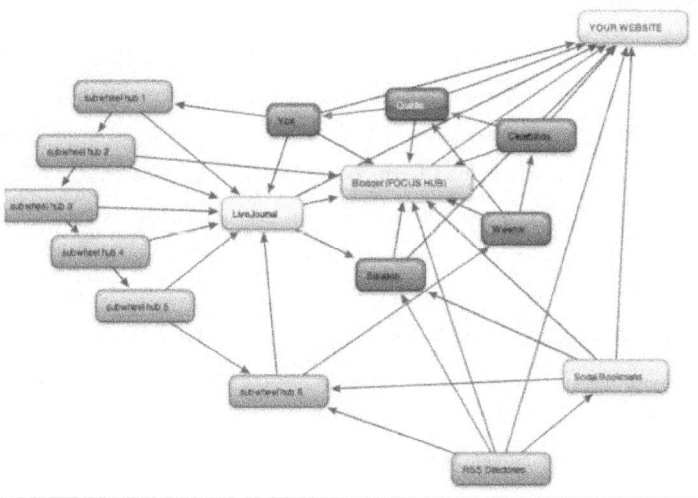

This is a visual of what a link wheel could look like. The focus is to always drive traffic back to your site, the center of all things.

Plan of Action: Optimize each page of your website independent of each other and co-dependent in a link wheel with great content. This means that each page of your site focuses on one thing that your audience wants to learn from you.

Plan of Action: Create a link wheel to connect your website to other relevant sites that hold a higher popularity score than your website.

Online Advertising & Pay Per Click

Pay per Click Campaign is also a marketing strategy that must be a consideration. When optimized for keywords that are specifically targeted to drive traffic that is typically going to your competitors

Pay per click (PPC) is an advertising model used on search engines, advertising networks, and content websites/blogs, where advertisers only pay when a user actually clicks on an ad to visit the advertiser's website. Advertisers bid on keywords they predict their target market will use as search terms when they are looking for a product or service. When a user types a keyword query matching the advertiser's keyword list, or views a page with relevant content, the advertiser's ad may be shown. These ads are called a "Sponsored link" or "sponsored ads" and appear next to or above the "natural" or organic results on search engine results pages, or anywhere a webmaster/blogger chooses on a content page.

Pay per click ads may also appear on content network websites. In this case, ad networks such as Google AdSense and Yahoo! Publisher Network attempt to provide ads that are relevant to the content of the page where they appear, and no search function is involved. Pay-per-click advertising is quickly becoming a necessary feature of any successful web presence. When used correctly, this form of advertising can prove to be extremely profitable, and not only boost online revenue, but also increase exposure and market awareness.

PPC – Pay-per-click search engines sell ranking by keyword in an auction format. If you want to have a high ranking you simply bid more for that particular word. These results appear at the top or side of the regular listings.

Main Engines – Yahoo Search Solutions and Google Adwords. Shopping PPCs or price comparison engines, include Shopping.com, Nextag.com, and Pricegrabber.com.

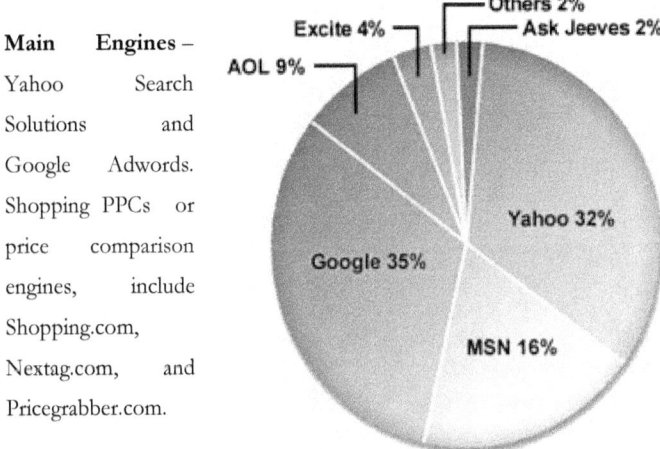

Benefits – Getting listed in a Directory or Spider engine can take weeks or months and getting a good ranking can take up to a year of trial and error. With a PPC listing you're up and running in under a week and you can get exactly the keyword and ranking you want.

<u>Plan of Action:</u> A minimal budget per month will allow you to determine what to focus on of the 20 most searched terms and increase your business. Use it wisely and only to boost your rankings

Website

Know How The Basics Fit Together And
Yes You Need A Website!

Website Development

Audience

Your website and its design has a subtle dance to complete, your preference and your audience's desires. Keeping in mind how your visitors will move and find what they want in balance with how you want the site to look. Websites are personal; it's your mark on the world in a very real way. The site must be user-friendly, clean aesthetics (not too busy), navigation simple and reliable. Less is more. Clean aesthetics lead to more conversion and a lower bounce rate.

Content

The information on the site needs to be updated to clearly and specifically tell those searching for your products what you are all about. The site can't be too vague to give the reader a good grasp of what is needed. The content on each page needs to be relevant to the terms being searched for. For example a wholesaler might enjoy just a list of items while a retail purchaser would like more descriptive information. The entire site needs to be relevant to and should target the area of the public that the website is concerned with.

If you find that your website has a high bounce rate (above 50%), you might be dealing with a problem of clarity, either in the message on your site, or in the expectations of the consumer not being met. Bounce Rate reflects how quickly someone visited your site and left, just like bouncing on a trampoline. The longer it takes for them to bounce, the more engaged they are.

Consumer expectation not being met is the same as if you sat down ravenous at the dinner table, having a great meal, but still feeling like something was missing. You are full, just not satisfied. Discerning that gap is the goal to decreasing your bounce rate.

While this section is short in this chapter, content is king and the most important strategy that you will ever employ. You are an authority in your business, so share you wealth of knowledge with the world and in turn it will increase your visibility and your rankings.

Landing Pages, Micro-Sites, & Banners

The information on the site needs to be updated to clearly and specifically tell those searching for your products what you are all about. A landing page is any page on your site that is specific to a single topic, content, or clear thought. For example, if a site is a restaurant, there should be a landing page about breakfast, appetizers, drinks, etc. So it's easy for your audience to find what they are looking for quickly. The harder you make it for them, the less likely they are to stay on your site much less walk in your doors.

Plan of Action: The site can't be too vague to give the reader and search engines good grasp that you are there. A site redesign for a simpler, more user friendly and ease of administration on site as well as onsite quick updates and picture adding should be considered.

Compatibility and Image Restrictions

Not all web browsers are alike. Chrome is different than Firefox, which is different from Internet Explorer. A standard outlining the compliance of a website or web browser is managed by the World Wide Web Consortium (W3C). Because of modern browsers, the compatibility of your website with the viewers is restricted…intentionally. It is meant to create brand loyalty to one particular browser over another. For instance, a website that is designed for the majority of web surfers will be limited to the use of valid XHTML 1.0 Strict or older, Cascading Style Sheets Level 1, and 1024x768 display resolution. This is because Internet Explorer is not fully W3C standards compliant with the modularity of XHTML 1.1 and the majority of CSS beyond 1. A target market of more alternative browser (e.g. Firefox and Opera) users allow for more W3C compliance and thus a greater range of options for a web designer.

Another restriction on webpage design is the use of different Image file formats. The majority of users can support GIF, JPEG, and PNG (with restrictions). Again Internet Explorer is the major restriction here, not fully supporting PNG's advanced transparency features, resulting in the GIF format still being the most widely used graphic file format for transparent images.

The other piece of the pie is that search engines, any search engine, is a machine and can't see the image itself. It uses a field called "ALT Text" for you to tell the machine what it is.

Plan of Action – Ensure pictures are .gif or jpeg files and create a multi-browser website compliant so that corporations and large businesses who use Internet Explorer exclusively are not left staring at big boxes with "X"'s in them because they can't see your images.

Ensure that the ALT text fields contain text information describing the image and your business so that when the image isn't displayed at the user's choice, they can still tell what it was and decide if they want to view the image.

Call to Action

People need to be told what to do when they land on your website or when they get an email. When considering the site's redesign, make sure to include a strong call to action to make a purchasing decision or convey your expertise. Part of a strong call to action for coaches include giving something away such as an e-book written in the language of the audience's pain and you have the solution. The verbiage needed for a good call to action is critical.

Plan of Action: Craft strong call to actions at every step of the process to lead your website visitors to a Yes in the buying cycle. Add "Join Our Newsletter" for latest deals & specials" to homepage. Craft a message for each page of your site, every email, every place that you are going to expose your brand to your audience. A Call to Action is telling your audience what to do at every step of the way

Key Issues in Website Design

<u>The appearance:</u> The graphics and text should include a single style that flows throughout, to show consistency. The style should be professional, appealing and relevant.

<u>The visibility:</u> The site must also be easy to find via most, if not all, major search engines and advertisement media.

<u>Plan of Actions:</u> Redesign the site with the goal of your audience in mind. Lots of picture but with the minimum 300 word count that is needed to best optimize the site to meet the needs of the search engine rankings. Several questions should be answered. Is an ecommerce online store beneficial to your consumers? Is is appropriate for your business to have a "Free Estimates" page?

Design and function of your website is critical. A plain website is often viewed as less than professional. We be work with designers to ensure that they create an aesthetically pleasing website that reflects the individual character of you & your brand as well as appealing to the customers you want to attract. Once the visitor clicks on the homepage it is important they continue to visit and navigate through the different pages and that the most important pages, the pages that convert to a sale are easy to find.

It's important to work closely with the website designers to create a search engine friendly website. Changes should be made quickly thus allowing your business the ability to react to local, regional and statewide changes in business. It is important that your website represent your vision and organization in a manner consistent with your businesses individual and corporate identity.

Determine the Site's Load Time

Google ranks a site highly only if the site has an adequate load time. If your site is slow, then your SEO is going to be poor. Here's how to determine the load time of your website:

Go to Pingdom.com, type in your URL, and click "test now."

Find Out the Domain Authority

Domain Authority (DA) is a number or score assigned to your site. The number is on a 100-point scale. The higher the number, the more authoritative your site is. Sites with higher DA scores get better search results. A site's DA increases with its age, SEO, and authoritative link backs. The DA is the single most important piece of information you need to score a site.

All you have to do is go to Open Site Explorer, type in your site's URL, and click "search."

DA   Rating

1-10   Poor. Your site is young and weak. You have a lot of growing to do.

11-20   Decent. Your site isn't stellar, but you're doing better. It would be beneficial to grow.

21-30   Fair. Your site shows signs of SEO, but there are many things you can and should do to improve.

31-40   Competitive. A lot of start-ups find themselves in this DA range. It's not bad, and you're beginning to get close to the sweet spot.

41-50   Good. Now you're getting somewhere. This is a nice place to be, and many good e-commerce sites find themselves squarely in this category.

51-60   Strong. As you swing out of the lower half of the scale, you're beginning to get much healthier. This is a good place to be.

61-70   Excellent. A DA at this level represents a great site with a lot of recognition, a lot of link backs, and a considerable amount of authority in its niche. Many .edus are in this space.

71-80   Outstanding. You're dominating in the SERPs and owning your niche.

81-90   Very outstanding. You're in the upper echelons of authority. You can consider yourself to have arrived at the top.

91-100 Rare. These sites are household names — Wikipedia, Facebook, New York Times, etc. Your site will probably never attain this level. Only a miniscule fraction of a percentage of sites on the Internet ever get this high.

Check for a sitemap.

Does your site have a sitemap? Sitemaps are a sign of an organized and easily indexable site, which is good for SEO. If you do not have one, you can create one easily using an online tool: https://www.xml-sitemaps.com/

This tool walks you through how to create a site map and what to do with it once you have created it. If your site is greater than 500 pages you'll need to pay for the sitemap to be created.

Check for meta content.

Make sure that you have the main meta components in place.

(Metatags Creation for the Homepage & Sub Pages – Every page is a landing page.)

The meta description is the little blurb that describes the content of the page listed in the search results. The meta description is only visible in the SERPs (and to users who view the source code of your pages), and the description cuts off after around 155 to 170 characters. While the meta description tag doesn't need to be optimized for search engines, it is nonetheless extremely valuable in that, to searchers, it acts as your page's ad copy. Therefore, it's important to ensure that each of your pages has a unique meta description, so that users can differentiate one page from the next in search results. Targeting the same keywords over and over again in multiple meta descriptions can result in keyword cannibalization and will confuse searchers as to which of your pages is most relevant to their search.

Again, the purpose of the meta description is to compel the searcher to click on your result in the SERPs; in this sense, it is foolhardy to stuff keywords into your description tag because, to a user, the description of your page will look spammy. During the development phase with your website, ensure that your meta information is useful and relevant to the site and aids in your marketing goals, rather than negatively impacting them.

<u>Plan of Action:</u> Optimize each page independently of each other and co-dependently in a link wheel.

Check for H-tags.

In addition to having the correct meta content, you should have header tags (H-tags) as well. Good SEO means having at least one H1 tag and, ideally, an H2, H3, and H4. Use the source code view to search for each of these elements.

I recommend using the CTRL +F feature to find each of these tags: H1, H2, H3, and H4.

Check for onsite content.

A site needs continual, updated content in order to rank well. It's very difficult to have sustained SEO without consistent content output.

If you're scoring your website, you probably already know whether or not you have an active blog.

If you're scoring a competitor's or client's website, it should be pretty easy to find a blog or content source. Navigate to the site's homepage, and look for a link to "Blog" or "Articles." Content marketing is important, so make your blog easy to find.

Social Score – Are you connected?

Coordinate Your Social Channels

As stated previously, your success will be limited if you treat each of your business's social media platforms as a stand-alone effort.

Start sharing information and establishing your brand's voice through your blog. Direct visitors through your sales funnel by interacting with your visitors.

Optimizing your website and blog for social media is as simple as adding a few simple key elements to your design.

Use this guide to start optimizing your business's social media channels. By following these simple steps you'll be setting yourself up for success!

Social Media

Know You Can Be Social Online

It is the Same As

Networking In Real Life

Social Media

Now that you have a plan and are armed with your analysis of your competitors, you are ready to take it to social media. Social media is any platform that allows you to talk with others.

"What You Did Yesterday isn't Going to Work Tomorrow." ~ Ginger Rockey-Johnson

Talking to your best customer and telling them how great you are is worthless. Your audience wants to listen to others, to share their experiences with others. People have an innate need to be heard and know that our voices matter. This is perhaps the single most influential thing that social media has done: It has made the shyest of people strong behind their computer monitors and as bold and brave as can be on their keyboards. Businesses didn't take social media platforms as seriously as they could have even five years ago, and some are still not on board yet.

If you are not convinced yet, just ask your customers where they find out about great deals, latest gossip, new restaurants, etc. Odds are that these topics were discussed during those coffee breaks and water cooler conversations, or on their phones, as they Instant Messaged on Facebook or texted with family and friends. The fact is that Americans spend an average of 37 minutes daily on social media, a higher time-consumer than any other major Internet activity, including email. As you can see, you'll have more exposure on social media than with any singular ad or email campaign alone.

Social Media is a Game Changer

Just when it seems that social media marketing has gone as far as it can, a new year begins, and the field continues to evolve. As business owners watch a New Year approach, many are wondering how they should adjust their content marketing efforts to match any industry changes in the next twelve months.

As you formulate a plan for your upcoming campaigns, it's important to take into account the social media environment we can expect over the course of 2015. Here are a few major changes to the social media landscape that experts are predicting next year.

Social media will continue to have significant impact in the future of marketing in 2015 for marketers and business owners. You now have the ability to reach out and communicate, on a personal level, with your target audience on a daily basis. ***This is a game changer for businesses engaging in marketing, sales, customer service and other business activities.*** *This is very powerful and has never been available with traditional marketing!*

In traditional marketing, consumers were left to figure out if they were buying the right product and angry when they bought into – or were suckered into – a clever marketing ploy.

> *"Make 'em laugh, or make 'em cry. Everything else is forgotten." ~ Ginger Rockey-Johnson*

Only two things in marketing work:
    Making them laugh
    Making them cry
Marketing is just networking in real life.

The two most influential things in life that you remember are the most Humorous moments and the most horrific moments.

If I ask you to tell me about a happy time in your life, a specific memory immediately comes to mind, and after that, your mind sprinkles in the details. That memory floods over you like waves, and you bubble over with excitement as the joy rushes in all over again.

If I ask you to tell me about a particularly sad time in your life, a specific memory comes to mind, and after that, your mind sprinkles in the details. It brings you to tears, and you can feel your heart pounding as that emotion rises to the top.

Marketing is the same way. Make them laugh, or make them cry, because everything else is forgotten. You are not invisible, so don't be a forgotten thought in your announcements, posts, etc. Deliver that WOW moment!

B2B Use of Social Media Will Only Grow In Years to Come

B2B is a term used to describe businesses that sell to other businesses. B2C is a term used to describe businesses that sell primarily to consumers. An example of a B2B business would be a marketing or advertising company. We sell to other businesses looking to get marketed. As opposed to a B2C type business such as a restaurant or daycare center, who serves consumers or direct users.

Nearly 94% of B2B executives surveyed in the USA during 2014 said they believe social media will be increasingly valuable to their companies in the coming year and almost 60% called that value significant. The thing to watch in the next 12 months is how well B2B marketers create a holistic approach to marketing by combining their new social tactics with the tried and true strategies of SEO and keeping pace with the consumers demand for personal attention.

Small And Large B2Bs Are More Social

The study also unearthed some interesting statistics on which B2Bs are leveraging social more. 88% of large companies (over $1 billion) and 80% of smaller B2Bs (under $50 million) engage in social media and while 68% of all companies intend to increase their social spending, only 46% of mid-sized businesses plan to follow suit.

Overall these numbers show that B2B marketers are figuring out how social can build their marketing effectiveness but many still have to overcome lack of management support and clarify which strategic combinations work best when it comes to merely having a social presence versus pursuing customer engagement and integrating paid media.

- Facebook
- Google+
- LinkedIn
- Twitter & Customer Service

The Top 4 Social Channels Are Getting B2B Action

A 2013 study showed Business to Business (B2B's) are extending their reach to the major social media channels. The numbers show how the top channels fared:

- Twitter 85%
- Facebook 74%
- LinkedIn 72%
- YouTube 69%
- Corporate Blogs 60%

83% of those surveyed said they use social media to communicate with target audiences and while Business to Consumer (B2C's) use social to generate sales, not surprisingly, B2Bs focus on lead generation.

Social Media Made Simple

I suggest that you begin by outlining clear goals for your social media marketing efforts, and figure out how you'll measure success. Once you've outlined your goals, let's look at ten great ways you can begin to leverage social media for your marketing efforts.

<u>Plan of Action:</u> Get in the game! Social Media presence is as critical today as a business card. Revamp your print collateral to include your social media presence.

E3 – The Real Power of Social Media

Social Media is about the 3E's – Entertainment, Engagement, and Education. The focus is not to be on selling your business. Nor is your focus to be about sharing your deals, coupons, and self-promotion efforts. Focus on your potential customers. What are they interested in? Talk about that as pieces of entertainment, to engage your audience, to educate people.

Entertainment

Too often, businesses post spammy content that is not of any entertainment value at all. People don't want to go home to read spam. Be value-adding with your content, as well as entertaining. Very few "entertaining" posts are as entertaining the second, third, or fourth time we see them. Typically, the comedy or the art in a post is short-lived, and even when it does have a lasting impact, it can be very difficult for the typical consumer to remember the link between the entertaining post and the initial page.

We should start by understanding that most marketing folks work to make us see interruptions (advertising) as not being interruptions. Take Hulu vs Netflix, for example. The platforms are exactly the same cost, and for the most part, the same content. However, Hulu employs interruption (advertising), while Netflix does not. What could make an advertisement not seem to be an interruption? When it makes us laugh? In the marketing arena, not everyone can agree on what is funny, or, more broadly, what is entertaining. It is entirely up to you and me – the consumers – as to what we find entertaining, which is why you must test and observe to see if this advertisement strategy works. These approaches have been the primary tools of the advertising industry to work toward rising above the simple annoyance of interruption discussed in the last section.

So, how can this form of advertisement be tested? It's simple; put an image out there that you find funny, and see how it flies with your audience. If they agree with you, your interaction (likes, follows, re-tweets, shares, pins, etc.) will go up. If your audience does not find the post funny, they won't respond. If it is way off topic, you most likely will get a few snide comments. Don't count this as a failure; just apologize and move on. "Tick. That one didn't work."

It's social. You can make a few mistakes, and it'll be fine. When in doubt, ask your audience. If you have worked at finding fans who want to talk with you because they love your brand, they will respond. Keep it light, and take note of what works and what doesn't, but most importantly, just get involved!

Engagement

Get to know your audience, and let them see the personality of "Brand You." They are going to experience that anyway once they engage with you in real life, so no change-ups!

Engagement is the same as being in a crowded room of people you don't know, and you are one of the last to arrive. You don't know anyone in the room, but you came to meet people. There are multiple people who are talking at the same time, and you have to select one person or a group of people to converse with.

Engagement in social media is the same. When you have a fan page, Twitter account or other platform, you select someone and start a conversation. At first, you just pick one person, and maybe you say a thank you, ask an opinion, strike up a conversation, etc. Be sincere. If he/she was a recent customer, you have more to say!

Education

You have something valuable to say. Educate your audience, and tell them what you know. If you are not sure what you have to say that is valuable, think of all the questions that customers ask you now. How many ask the same question over and over again? That is what you can educate them on.

I once had a client who owned an embroidery store. He said, "There's nothing about embroidery that is interesting to others. I just want more customers." Well, he soon discovered that he had plenty to say, and he soon became an expert in how well logos are designed. If it could be embroidered, it could be reproduced anywhere. You have tons to share with the world, no matter your area of expertise.

I believe that the best strategy to educate your potential customers is to blog and share that on your social media platforms. Remember to share educational content, as well as entertaining content, and point everything back to your blog, so they can see who you are and what you are about.

Grow your audience and talk with them, not at them. Too

many times, we forget that the Internet is meant to draw people closer together. It is the one opportunity to connect with and get to know people you do not already know.

Why would you go to a party and never talk to anyone? The same thing can be said for social media and your business. Why are you there if you aren't going to attempt to get to know them in hopes of filling your sales funnel and meeting them one day?

Point everything back to your site, and sprinkle in information about your business and what solutions you have to their problems. It's all about engagement. Get in the game!

Exposure is Everything

Like most small businesses and organizations, you probably have two wishes:

- To find new customers, members and connections.
- To get repeat business, participation and referrals from them.

Here's the secret: **engagement marketing.** It's the way to make sure your interactions with customers last longer than "one and done." It ensures that a passing interest in you becomes a longer-lasting relationship, one they're eager to tell others about, creating a cycle of more business and involvement. We can help you develop your Engagement Marketing Plan, so that you can make repeat business and word-of-mouth happen by doing the following:

- Engaging with your existing audience.
- Leveraging that engagement to create social visibility that's easily seen and shared—and easy for others to get in on.

Engagement Marketing's concepts are simple. You probably know very well, however, that as small business, you often lack the time and/or skills to develop and execute a business- building marketing strategy.

Text is No Longer Just Enough

The term "social networking" now encompasses a wide variety of options. No longer are users simply typing out a short status update about what they're doing. Today, people are networking using photos, videos, check-ins, and more—all in an effort to interact with others. In 2015, businesses of all sizes will discover the power of social media sites, like Instagram and Vine, to creatively market content.

Viral Explodes

The power of going viral isn't lost on marketers, but creating content so compelling (or outrageous) that audiences share it with others is extremely difficult. As content marketers struggle to go further than anyone has gone before, those attempts will likely become lost in a sea of similar content.

To stand out in the social media world, successful brands will remain true to their customer bases, while also being innovative and unique. Customer engagement will become more important than ever, as businesses realize the importance of reaching out to people on an individual basis, rather than sending out one generic message intended to win over the masses.

Measurement and Analysis

We've only begun to unleash the power of all of the information that exists about consumers. In 2015, businesses will spend more time than ever tracking click-throughs, conversions, and other behaviors on their social media sites, using this information to steer their campaigns. In fact, Big Data Analytics is on most lists of "top tech trends to watch" this year, showing how important statistical reporting will be in everything businesses do going forward.

For 2015, businesses will also realize the importance of setting aside part of the annual marketing budget for reporting. Mobile will also become a larger part of marketing analysis, with businesses investigating which of their efforts are working and which should be discarded.

As social media continues to be a large part of many consumers' daily lives, marketers are looking for new ways to engage and excite their audiences. As 2015 begins, businesses are sophisticated enough to realize how social media trends are shifting, in order to better create campaigns that pop.

PINTEREST

SOCIAL SITE THAT IS ALL ABOUT DISCOVERY

LARGEST OPPORTUNITIES

USERS ARE: ♂ 32% MALE ♀ 68% FEMALE

70 MILLION ACTIVE USERS

TWITTER

MICRO BLOGGING SOCIAL SITE THAT LIMITS EACH POST TO **140** CHARACTERS

LARGEST PENETRATION

5,700 TWEETS HAPPEN EVERY SECOND

BUT SPREADING SLOWLY AND STEADILY

560 MILLION ACTIVE USERS

FACEBOOK

SOCIAL SHARING SITE THAT HAS **1 BILLION** USERS WORLDWIDE

LARGEST OPPORTUNITIES

COMMUNICATING WITH CONSUMERS IN A NON-OBTRUSIVE WAY

USERS SHARE **2.5 BILLION** PIECES OF CONTENT EACH DAY

1 BILLION ACTIVE USERS

INSTAGRAM

SOCIAL SHARING SITE ALL AROUND PICTURES AND NOW 15 SECOND VIDEOS

MANY BRANDS ARE PARTICIPATING THROUGH THE USE OF **#HASHTAGS** AND POSTING PICTURES CONSUMERS CAN RELATE TO

MOST FOLLOWED BRAND IS MTV

150 MILLION ACTIVE USERS

GOOGLE+

SOCIAL NETWORK BUILT BY GOOGLE THAT ALLOWS FOR BRANDS AND USERS TO BUILD CIRCLES

NOT AS MANY BRANDS ACTIVE, BUT THE ONES THAT ARE TEND TO BE A GOOD FIT WITH A GREAT FOLLOWING

GROWING RAPIDLY WITH **925,000** NEW USERS EVERY DAY

400 MILLION ACTIVE USERS

LINKEDIN

BUSINESS ORIENTED SOCIAL NETWORKING SITE

BRANDS THAT ARE PARTICIPATING ARE CORPORATE BRANDS GIVING POTENTIAL AND CURRENT ASSOCIATES A PLACE TO NETWORK & CONNECT

79% OF USERS ARE 35 OR OLDER

240 MILLION ACTIVE USERS

Social Media Optimization

In Social Media Examiner's 2013 End of Year Report, it was shown that marketers now place **very high value** on social media marketing. While this report was for 2014, it is relevant for 2015.

- 86% of marketers stated that social media is important for their businesses.
- 89% of marketers stated that increased exposure was the number one benefit of social media marketing.

These are the definitive benefits of social media marketing that are listed:

1. Increased exposure
2. Increased traffic
3. Developed loyal fans
4. Generated leads
5. Improved search ranking
6. Grew business partnerships
7. Reduced marketing expenses
8. Improved sales
9. Provided marketplace insight

The success gap is widening between businesses that are using social media in an informal, ad hoc manner and those taking a **more planned, strategic approach.**

Businesses that use social media strategically are more satisfied with the results than ad hoc users, who are more skeptical about the value of social media. Businesses that use social media as part of a planned corporate approach are 1.5 to 2 times more likely to anticipate revenue growth than ad hoc users.

Much has changed over the last two year in social media, and this change will continue in 2015..

Sharing is Caring!

I know this sounds basic, but make sure your website, blog, and email newsletter include social "share" buttons for people to **easily share your content on ALL their social networks.**

Add your social network links on your email signature.

What Will Social Media Do For Your Business?

Making social media a priority for your business will allow your business to do the following:

- Be found!
- Establish a stronger brand.
- Boost sales.
- Share expertise and knowledge.
- Tap into the wisdom of customers.
- Interact with customers, and receive valuable customer feedback.
- Gain free advertising. Satisfied customers talk about your company, and this is the strongest word-of-mouth-marketing.
- Build a community.

Overview

Social media and social media optimization is here to stay.

What is the Best Social Media Channel for your Business?

Determine the top channels for your business from the information gathered above. There are many options, including Facebook, Twitter, LinkedIn, blogging, YouTube, Google+, Pinterest, SlideShare, Yelp.

Do not spread yourself too thin. It's better to have a strong, consistent presence on one channel than a weak, inconsistent presence on two or more.

In this section we'll look at each platform, what you need to do for exposure, dimensions of cover photo sizes, and trends for 2015.

Coordinate Your Social Channels

Your success will be limited if you treat each of your business's social media platforms as a stand-alone-effort. All of your networks should work in unison to better your chances of success. Think of your website as your brand's home base. Push customers to your site by coordinating your social efforts. In this way, you are leading them to a place where they can buy your products or services.

Start sharing information and establishing your brand's voice through your blog. Direct visitors through your sales funnel by interacting with your visitors.

Optimizing your website and blog for social media is as simple as adding a few simple key elements to your design.

Make sure you display your social icons prominently in your header or sidebar if you want visitors to follow all your different social profiles. Link the social icons on your website to each of your social profiles, so that readers and potential customers can follow you right away.

Always integrate sharing buttons to your pages and posts, in order to provide "share friendly" content. People want to share content that they find interesting or valuable with their friends and followers. By not using sharing buttons, you open up the opportunity for your visitors (a.k.a., potential customers) to click away, ultimately reducing your chances of reaching a wider audience.

Some Powerful Stats and Information from 2013

Social media is now the top Internet activity! Americans spend an average of 37 minutes daily on social media, a higher time-spend than any other major Internet activity, including email.

Facebook is still the leading social media network and continues to grow. Here are the latest **facts and figures**:

- Facebook now has 1.26 billion users.
- Facebook averages 1.23 billion monthly active users.
- There are 128 million daily active Facebook users in the US.
- Facebook averages 945 million monthly active mobile users.
- Facebook usage is highest in North America and has 59% of all Internet users in North America as active users. Google+ only achieves 15%, and Twitter 25%.

Google+ is boasting to be the second largest social network at just over 35%, with Facebook still dominating at 70%. Keep in mind that a Google+ account is mandatory whenever a person creates a new Gmail account. This is pushing up the account ownership stats. However, no other social network has Google's web assets leverage. Google treat Google+ as a webpage and gives it priority over most other properties on the web.

YouTube is now more popular than cable television and reaches more adults than any cable network reaches. In the United States, the number of people who watch television has fallen behind the number of people who watch YouTube on a regular basis. This makes it clear that televised content is undergoing a decline, while online consumption of video is on the incline. Many companies have taken advantage of this by releasing their ads or marketing campaigns on YouTube first before they debut on TV. Take, for example, many of the 2014 Super Bowl XLVIII ads (like <u>Budweiser</u>) that were released on YouTube before the big game and were rewarded with triple YouTube views.

LinkedIn is still the largest professional business network and continues to grow, but not at the pace of Pinterest, Google+, or Twitter. This platform is for the serious minded business professional and C-Suite Executives. The site is organized very much like a resume so caution is the word here.

Terms of Service require you to only have one account and that account should reflect the public image you want to cast forward. That one brand and the experience that says you have what it takes. Don't show irrelevant past experiences or job history that doesn't matter to what you are doing today. You also do not want such a variety on your profile that it looks like you are the Jack of all trades and master of none. In other words this is not a site where your business card of the day, week, month, or even year rotates. Decide what you are going to be and stick with it. Too often we meet people in real life and they have a rotating gambit of business cards.

Pinterest is currently the fastest-growing social network. The visual web is driving the rise of Pinterest and Tumblr, with growth rates of 88% and 74% respectively over the last 12 months. Pinterest is also one of the **leading referral sources** for organic traffic, which is good for high search rankings.

What were two key factors driving the social web in 2013 and 2014?

Mobile – The number of people accessing the Internet via a mobile phones. Phablets (larger phones with tablet capabilities), or tablets increased by 60.3% to 96.4 % in the last two years. In the USA, there are now 101 million daily mobile users.

Older user adoption – On Twitter, the 35-54 year age bracket is the fastest-growing demographic, with a 79% growth rate since 2012. The fastest-growing demographic on Facebook's and Google+'s networks are the 55 to 74 year age bracket, at 56% and 46% respectively. So, maybe that's the reason your parents and grandparents aren't visiting that much anymore; they are too busy on Facebook and Twitter!

The **top challenges** businesses have in using social media are as follows:

- Lack of time
- Inability to measure value
- Difficulty integrating social media with other business activities
- Lack of budget

I absolutely agree that these are legitimate struggles, and I hear it first-hand from many of my clients. However, these challenges can be overcome, if social media is planned and done strategically!

Social Media Channels – Which One to Choose??

Business owners should pay attention to which social platforms help them reach their goals with their individual relevant audiences, whether that's generating sales or greater visibility. Part of my job **is helping business owners decide** which networks are best for their businesses.

Here are the most popular ones:

- Facebook
- Twitter
- YouTube
- LinkedIn
- Google+
- Pinterest
- Instagram
- Slideshare presentation sharing

And, of course, blogging is key!

Integrate!

Social media is not an end unto itself. It MUST be **integrated and work hand-in-hand** with all of your other marketing and PR initiatives, which should be **continued** to reach all of your marketing touch points and your ultimate success. These can include the following:

1. Email marketing and growing your email list
2. Search engine optimization
3. Event marketing (speaking and networking)
4. Direct mail
5. Online ads (Google Adwords)
6. Printed display ads
7. Sponsorships
8. Mobile Marketing
9. Radio/TV Ads

Facebook

There are more than 800 million people using Facebook every day. This platform offers more than just a way to stay connected to friends and family; it is an essential tool in the B2B marketing toolbox. Facebook allows your business to be available to people on a trusted, popular platform, so that prospects can see "real" people (friends, family, or colleagues) interacting with you and your brand. This sets the stage for you to build stronger, more immediate relationships with them.

However, businesses need to strike that critical balance of offering content that is relevant and that add value, as opposed to content that is simply entertaining.

- Does this help our brand's likeability?
- Is this interesting, engaging, useful content?

Posting only for the sake of posting can actually hurt your chances of being seen. The second you post something that is not engaging or relevant, EdgeRank will stop amplifying your posts and placing them in your fans' newsfeeds (more on that below).

Facebook pages can help your company build awareness, share enthusiasm, create loyalty, strengthen inbound marketing, and promote peer-to-peer sharing. First, let's break down the elements of a Facebook page and how you can take advantage of this resource.

Facebook's New Timeline: What You Need to Know

Facebook began rolling out another new timeline format in March & October 2014. Here's how it better serves B2B companies:

- The "scrapbook" style allows you to prominently display key snapshots of your business's brand and marketing focus, while also giving you the ability to tell a story and to highlight your company's milestones.
- Interactions, comments on fan pages, and "likes" about your company appear in a user's timeline. "Likes" will also appear in a box at the top of the user's page, keeping you prominently at the top of your audience's minds.
- The ticker shows a live stream of friends' activities and conveniently allows users to "like" a page without leaving their own newsfeeds. In other words, Facebook users can easily see when their friends are interacting with or commenting about your brand, and they can do the same.
- The timeline offers more branding and lead-capture options. The large cover image presents plenty of room for your branding, marketing images, and calls to action, so you can capture the eye of a potential customer and get him or her to visit your page.

EdgeRank Explained

The content you create and share is your "make-or-break" component on Facebook. To get the most out of your Facebook page and presence, your posts' appearance on your fans' newsfeeds is essential. This is where EdgeRank becomes important. EdgeRank is Facebook's algorithm that personalizes users' newsfeeds and inserts posts that it thinks will interest them. In very simplified terms, if users (or their friends) are interacting with your company/brand on a fairly frequent basis, you show up; if not, you get dropped.

When it comes to Facebook marketing, you can use two metrics to measure your success: engagement rate and the "people are talking about this" rating:

1) Your engagement rate can be determined by dividing your total "likes" and comments by your total number of fans (likes + comments/total # of fans). That's why your posts need to be engaging and spark a reaction. A high engagement rate helps you build your EdgeRank and gets you seen more often.

2) Your "people are talking about this" rating is basically your "buzz" metric. It measures who's talking about you or your posts on their pages and can be found in your page's Facebook insights, as well as on your page. For example, on Marketo's Facebook page, the "talking about this" number is located on the profile page, just under the cover photo and the chart below that is trending that number. It basically shows when Marketo's activities in the real, virtual, or social worlds are sparking conversation on Facebook.

The next logical question is, "How do we increase our interaction and sharing?" To boost interaction, businesses need to post more often and engage their consumers in a two-way dialogue. More than 70% of interactions occur during the first hour after a post is made. Keep your interactions up by posting more often and by being online and available right after you post. In other words, don't post and then immediately go to bed. Also, keep in mind that a post posed as a "question" tends to drive more interaction than one written as a statement.

Things You Must Know about Facebook

It's not the Fan Count that matters…How to See and be Seen

Remember that Facebook's EdgeRank algorithm rewards pages in the newsfeed based on the number of interactions a page receives, not your fan count (engagement). An interaction can be defined as a summary of "likes," posts, or comments about the page.

To show up in as many users' top newsfeeds as possible, your content must be fresh, engaging, current, and compelling. Then, it becomes a cycle; you post content that gets "Likes" and comments, and your future content appears in the newsfeeds of those that "liked" and commented on earlier content. Don't forget this: As prospects interact with you through "Likes," reposts, or shares, you should be tracking engagement.

Visual content such as pictures, videos, infographs, etc, are critical to sharing and maintaining EdgeRank. On Facebook, people love sharing images, so you want to make sure that you are leveraging something that is visually stimulating. To get the best results you should use a variety of images to get engagement from your followers.

Facebook Groups

The Group feature is useful for demonstrating your company's passion for a topic, as it gathers like-minded people to share ideas. The best part is that the more people join your group, the more it gets promoted to their friends and networks, increasing the group's popularity and growth. Creating a Facebook group is a great way for businesses to create awareness, increase inbound links, and foster loyalty.

Facebook Lists

Facebook launched this feature in response to Google+'s circles, so it functions in a very similar way. You can subscribe to and organize lists for different topics or influencers you want to follow. As an example, you might have one list for social media influencers and another list for competitors. Through lists, you can easily view and post to select groups or a company, which makes it easier for you to monitor and engage.

Facebook Promoted Posts

Promoted posts show up in the newsfeed of all your fans and are visible to their friends as well. It becomes a sponsored story that is seen by more people than a regular post, so be sure that when you do choose to promote a post, it is strong, current, and compelling. It is pretty safe to say that businesses will never be able to compete with posts that are strictly entertainment-based or for social purposes only. However, by using this promoted post feature, you can call attention to posts that you believe will generate the most impact.

Facebook suggests using promoted posts for any of the following to get you more exposure:

1. Unique, vibrant, and interesting photos and videos
2. Offers
3. Exclusive events or news
4. Questions

We found the magic formula for promoted posts to be this: Clever messaging with a fun visual, all tied back to a strong offer or piece of content.

Facebook Ads

While your Facebook ads need to appeal to your audience, think outside the box. Use eye-catching pictures and compelling language. Remember that you're competing for attention in an already noisy environment.

Facebook Apps

Before the timeline changes took place, you could capture "likes" via your welcome page by gating your content and encouraging users to "like" your page for access to this exclusive content. This has gone away with the timeline format. Now, Facebook gives you the option to feature up to twelve apps. Four of these apps are shown by default, with the remaining apps under the fold and only visible by clicking and expanding the tab on the right. Although you cannot move the photo app as the default, you can control which other three apps show above the fold. It's important to optimize these three, and rotate them frequently with fresh offers.

Allowing you to change the apps appearing above the fold is one of the most interactive and engaging portions of the timeline and your best chance to showcase a call to action or offer that will convert. Take this into consideration when selecting the display images of your apps. Consider the image a small advertisement, rather than an image.

Google +

Google+ is Necessary…Not

In its early days, Google+ struggled to get noticed in an overcrowded social media marketplace. Both businesses and consumers tended to disregard the platform, seeing it as just another site to keep up with.

2014 has made it clear, however, that Google will not let one of its services go down without a fight. Marketers are realizing that in order to get the search engine results they desire, Google+ membership is a must. For that reason, 2015 will likely be the year that Google+ users begin growing their circles and posting content through the service.

However long they are around, Google+ has quickly becoming an essential part of any business's social media strategy. Boasting 90 million users, this social network is going to grow very quickly, as Google is making a Google+ account mandatory for all Gmail users. Google + is also playing a major role in SEO by making it easier for marketers to show up in search results.

An essential (but often overlooked) important first step, the "about" page is a fantastic opportunity to give a quick overview of what your business is all about. You can also link back to specific pages and services from this page, directing potential customers to the most important pages on your website.

It's important to have a balance of marketing savvy copy that is also SEO friendly. Make sure to include information that searchers will want to know about your company. Take advantage of the fact that

Google+ allows you to use bullets in your description, which makes it simple to create an easy-to-read list of your products and services. You can also include links to specific pages, as well as a contact form. Test and track different variations to see what works best for your business.

Google Events

Google recently announced the "events" feature, which allows G+ users to send out customized invitations to anyone, regardless of whether or not they are also G+ users. It syncs beautifully with Google Calendar and shows up automatically when a user confirms for an event.

In addition to sending out invites to webinars, work functions, parties, etc., Google Events can also send out invites for Google Hangouts. This could be the catalyst that gets your business on board to start using Hangouts or increase the awareness and attendance of the ones you are already hosting.

The "Party mode" feature of Events allows everyone in attendance to instantly upload pictures to the same album using the Google+ mobile app, creating a living, real-time photo journal of a specific time and place. You can then show the photos off in chronological order as a slideshow, all within Google+.

Circles

This functionality allows a marketer to segment his or her followers. Unlike other social networks, through Circles, marketers can develop personas and communicate highly segmented messages to each audience. This allows you to have a more authentic dialogue with your key prospects.

Hangouts

Use Google+ Hangouts for video conferencing. Again, the beauty here is that it is highly integrated with other Google applications. So, if you use Google apps for your business, Hangouts can be a quick and easy way to connect teams and get some face time with a prospect.

The ease at which you can share photos and images with others is a huge boon for B2B companies. It lets you record and increase the visibility of company events, industry conferences, user groups, and more. Prospects and customers love visual content, so make sure you are consistently using images in your marketing mix. Why are photos king? Here are our top reasons why you should use photos and images as part of your marketing campaigns.

- Appeals to Emotions: Visual content appeals to the viewer's emotions in a way that text is unable to do. Thanks to the simplicity of photo and image sharing applications, text is an afterthought.

- Creates Intimacy: Photos help open the personal side of your company. Now customers and prospects can relate to your brand message via photos, without a plethora of emails.

- Engages: Photo and image sharing applications provide the perfect opportunity for your business to engage customers in a fun way through contests and other image-centric campaigns.

Twitter

In 2007, Twitter began as what many considered to be a flash-in-the-pan social media outlet, but as of 2011, Twitter had over 200 million registered users and is now one of the ten most popular sites on the Internet – anything but a passing phase. Companies that lack a strategic, lead-generating plan of attack for their Twitter accounts are losing out on access to a huge potential customer base and the opportunity to showcase themselves as social savvy, relevant businesses. Being followed on Twitter is an incredibly strong signal of online affinity for your business. These self-selected prospects are indicating an active interest in your brand and are asking to hear more from you.

Think of Twitter as the water cooler for B2B marketers. It's a vibrant community in which businesses can prospect leads and congregate as thought leaders to discuss relevant industry topics. B2B marketers are always striving to provide good content in an easily, digestible, and timely format. On Twitter, it is easy to quickly compose Tweets and messages aimed at those interested in your company or product (Caveat: words of caution about this to follow).

Twitter happens to be one of our most effective prospecting channels. We use it to get the word out to customers about specific product offerings and as a forum for potential customers to discover and learn more about us and what we offer.

Twitter Following

Becoming someone's follower on Twitter accomplishes four goals:

- You identify Twitter accounts that will be relevant and interesting to you, your organization, and your industry.
- You let people know that you're on Twitter, and encourage them to follow you back.
- You associate yourself with a specific group of industry experts and thought leaders, and demonstrate your interest in the space.
- Twitter is a great platform for engagement, so once you follow someone on Twitter, you can work on starting a conversation.

Tips for Following

- Find people to follow by importing your contact databases using tools that Twitter provides. Then, broaden this action by following those that your followers are following – where relevant. Be sure to also follow people that your competitors are following.
- Do a search for experts in the field who are tweeting. You can find people to follow on sites like Wefollow.com or Twibes.com.
- If possible, try to make sure to follow back relevant people and companies that are following you. You don't want to upset prospects, customers, or partners by not following them!
- Twitter provides easy search functionality, so that you can find people who are talking about your company and your industry. Spend some time trying out different searches and hashtags that are relevant to your business. Once you find the people who are contributing most to the conversation, start following them.
- Read the tweets of those you follow, and search for tweets on keywords relevant to your product or service. Twitter client applications, such as TweetDeck, Hootsuite, and Seesmic, are useful for organizing your Twitter feeds, managing multiple microblogging accounts, and posting or scheduling posts from multiple users.
- Create lists. By creating a list, you can easily segment people whom you are following. As an example, you can create one list for hot prospects, one for customers, and one for competitors.

Tweetchats

A Twitter chat is a public conversation on Twitter, based around a unique hashtag. The hashtag allows you to follow the discussion and easily participate in it. Most Twitter chats are usually recurring and on specific topics, but some are also based around special events. Hosting a Twitter chat is an amazing way to engage with your fans and followers. In addition, this is a great way to better understand and grow your community and to promote your brand and business.

What's Awesome? Unlike other chats, participants are encouraged to agree or disagree and really get to the root of the issue. Hashtag also features the question of the day.

Retweet:

- Always use a URL shortener, such as Bit.ly. They are also often built into other tools, such as Hootsuite and Tweetdeck. You only have 140 characters, so make them count!
- Keep tweets below 140 characters and ideally under 100 characters. This makes retweeting easier to do.
- The symbol # on Twitter is known as a hashtag. These tags are used to affiliate a tweet with a certain topic and can be useful for tracking social marketing campaigns and connecting with customers. You can develop your own hashtags to try promoting a viral following for a specific topic or campaign.
- Avoid the temptation to use tools that send automatic, direct messages. These types of messages are often construed as spam and may cause people to "unfollow" you.
- You can also engage Twitter followers and influencers by including an @mention in your tweets. You can do this when you post content you think will resonate with an influencer. An

easy format to follow is tweeting with a link to relevant content and then including the @mention at the end of the tweet.
- Use Twitter lists to segment users by interest, or group together brand advocates and your favorite twitter users. Keep in mind that when you add a user to a public list, they are notified, and the list is open and searchable to all users. A private list, which may be used for competitors, is only visible to you.
- Use Twitter during events and to promote things like contests.
- A great way to engage your Twitter followers is to create a contest that asks followers to contribute in some way. You want your Twitter feed to be a mix of Tweets you've created, as well as replies and retweets.

Promoted Tweets in Timelines

A Twitter strategy we have used with great success is launching promoted tweets in timelines targeted to followers and users who are similar to our followers. Our promoted tweets contain timely and engaging content, like contests for trips to industry events and links to thought-leadership pieces. Every promoted tweet that we run goes to a gated resource page. We set up a series of three tweets per campaign and rotate them accordingly. For timelines, we run three tweets on one campaign for three days at a time.

Promoted Tweets in Search

For search tweets, we run two offers every two weeks, with three different tweets, focusing on fifteen keywords and five countries.

We have found, through trial and error that it's more about the offer than about the money spent. Fresh, relevant content offers with the right messaging yields CTRs of up to 17%, with a cost-per-prospect coming in at around $14 each. This, of course, will vary based on your offer and the relevancy of your content.

We always see significant spikes in relevant tweets during industry events. We decided to capitalize on that and use promoted tweets in search results during key B2B conference dates. This allowed us to become part of relevant conversations when the conversations are hot. By targeting event-specific hashtags and relevant keywords, like "B2B" and "lead management," we are where we need to be at prime lead-generating moments. Being a part of real-time conversations means pouncing on real-time opportunities.

Influencer Marketing on Twitter

Twitter is a fantastic platform to learn who your influencers are. Because Twitter is designed for quick exchanges of information and shares, you can start to keep track of who is re-tweeting your content and engaging in conversations. Remember to reach out to your top sharers to create relationships. They may be interested in doing a guest blog, or allowing you to do a guest blog on their site. The more you engage directly with your top influencers, the more they will continue to promote your content.

Messaging

To some, this may sound backward or surprising, but do not use Twitter only to promote your company. Sure, calling out your company's new ebook or webcast is an important part of your tweeting, but if you never contribute to the conversations taking place, if you never offer something personal or fun or funny, you are missing the prime opportunity unique to Twitter. Twitter is about building relationships; it is about reciprocity. Engage, and be engaged. Be a part of the flow of information. Don't be a broken record repeatedly rattling off the company's tagline. It's in your best interest to pay attention to what your customers and prospective customers are tweeting about and to respond accordingly.

Remember, your content should create value and, ultimately, be helpful to your network. In B2B marketing, retweeting material that will be helpful to your network is good, but writing your own informational material is even better. If your network (specifically, customers and prospective buyers) benefits from something you tweet about, they will remember you and your business.

Here is that word of caution mentioned earlier: As with anything, a little self-promotion is good for business, but if your entire tweet history is only about you and your company, you've got it wrong. Keep in mind the 4-1-1 rule.

The 4-1-1 rule for Twitter was popularized by Tippingpoint Labs and Joe Pulizzi, founder of Junta42 and the Content Marketing Institute. For every one self-serving tweet, you should re-tweet one relevant tweet, and, most importantly, share four pieces of relevant content written by others.

What's great about this approach is that it lets you engage in the conversation, build awareness, and keep in touch with your followers, without coming across as pushy or too "me" focused. As you plan out the cadence of updates you'll send, try scheduling four educational or entertaining tweets, mixed with one "soft promotion" (e.g., prompting the audience to attend an event) and one "hard promotion" (e.g., prompting the audience to download a free trial or apply for an account).

Quick Tip

You will also want to make sure that your Twitter handle is short, as you only have 140 characters to complete your post. Having a short Twitter handle will help your followers when they re-tweet you.

LinkedIn

As a leading social networking site for professionals, LinkedIn is perfect for B2B organizations, as the focus is on education, work history, companies, and professional interests.

Build Out Your Company's LinkedIn Profile

Companies can build a profile on LinkedIn that showcases products, employee networks, blog posts, upcoming events, and status updates. Much like Twitter or Facebook, users on Linkedin can follow your profile to learn more about your company. You can also post jobs on Linkedin, making it a great venue for recruiting top candidates. Here are some tips to get started on creating your LinkedIn page:

- Give a voice to your products: The new "Products" page allows you to assign members of your organization to different product offerings, so prospects know exactly with whom to get in touch. This is a great way to start conversations between top prospects and product managers, sales staff, and support staff within your organization.

- Recommendations: After you create your "Products and Services" page, you can begin using recommendations. This gives current customers or employees a forum to recommend your products and services to others.
- Videos: You can now post videos directly to LinkedIn on your "Products and Services" page. Place them next to product descriptions to get the most value and visibility.

Offers

The "Products and Services" page now has a promo box. This is a great place to include contests, promotions, and discounts. Use this area to drive additional traffic to your website. Use "Shared Connections" to make introductions into companies you want to target.

One of the primary capabilities of LinkedIn is its ability to connect you to a larger network of people through your existing connections. LinkedIn shows you the degrees of separation between you and other LinkedIn users and allows you to connect with those outside of your direct network through introductions. Use LinkedIn introductions as a form of target account marketing, by identifying potential prospects and asking your own contacts to introduce you.

Build a LinkedIn Group Around Your Company's Specializations and Core Competencies.

The "Groups" feature is a great way to demonstrate thought leadership around a specific area – and to gain insight into the pain points of potential customers. Encourage customers to use this as a forum for discussions, and assign someone to monitor your group. The monitor should post responses and keep the conversation going. LinkedIn groups make it easy for B2B companies to locate potential customers. Simply make a list of keywords that relate to your prospects or the industries you target, and run a search for any LinkedIn groups related to these keywords. Once you find the right groups, participate in discussions, ask questions and make connections.

Encourage Your Employees to Participate.

LinkedIn is a great venue for your employees to promote both your brand and their own personal brands. Employee contributors should post your company blogs on their LinkedIn status updates and join relevant groups. The more evangelists you have on LinkedIn, the more opportunities you have to become a thought leader in your space.

LinkedIn and SEO

LinkedIn is fantastic for SEO and having properly optimized pages, as both company and employee can boost SEO and organic visibility. Encourage employees to optimize their pages by using the following quick tips:

- Include a professional headshot.
- Include keywords in job position titles.
- Link to the company blog under "Websites."
- Add a Twitter handle.
- Claim a unique URL, and then drop it into email signatures.
- Write a summary in the first person, and think of it as a

"greatest hits collection." Include keywords, and add a bit of your own personality.
- Under "Specialties," include a line that lists all of your skills – one on top of the other – to make your profile easy to read.
- Make sure to add plenty of skills in the "Skills" section
- Move your recommendations closer to the top.

LinkedIn Advertising

Like Facebook ads and Promoted tweets, LinkedIn advertising is a great way to get your message across to the right audience. LinkedIn ads work like PPC, and because LinkedIn holds valuable demographic information, this may be a great platform for you to reach your target audience. When you set up a LinkedIn profile, you put in information such as title, role, company, work experience, etc., and LinkedIn can use that information to help very specifically target advertising.

Create ads that work for your target audience. When you develop an ad on LinkedIn, you will be asked to select your demographics based on role, title, industry, geography, and a variety of other criteria. Remember to think about your keywords when working in each demographic. An ad geared toward a practitioner will be different than an ad geared toward an executive level prospect.

Think about your call to action. As with your ad copy, you want to make sure that your call to action is appropriate to your target audience. If it is a piece of content, think about whether your target audience will resonate with that content.

Additionally, make sure that you are utilizing one call to action per ad, so that you give your prospect clear direction.

Other Important LinkedIn Tips:

Make sure your profile is as complete as possible. Fill out as much information as you can about what you do and why you have joined the site. Additionally, it's optional to add a picture, as it's good to be able to put a face to a name and "humanize" your profile.

Try to get recommendations from others that include positive comments about your company. These comments contribute to social validation about your organization when people view your page. Do this for both personal profiles and for your company profile, as it allows for reviews as well.

Pay attention to the network updates you receive from LinkedIn, as they share important updates about your connections and can hold the key to new business opportunities for you and your company.

Use LinkedIn Answers to ask thought-provoking questions, or become an "expert" by providing valuable answers and demonstrating thought leadership. LinkedIn Answers are a great way for you to showcase your interests, expertise, and problem-solving capabilities to entire networks of people, which can indirectly drive interest in your company and new business.

Promote events on LinkedIn. The events section of LinkedIn allows event organizers to post events and encourages those planning to attend to RSVP for the event. This promotes additional visibility and encourages sharing.

Pinterest

Pinterest is a virtual scrapbook or pinboard that allows users to share and organize visual imagery. A user can pin anything from around the web, and other users can re-pin their images. Users organize their Pinterest pages by categorizing content on boards.

For businesses, Pinterest can be a way to curate visual content, such as infographics, videos, company culture, and even blog posts. Pinterest can help promote creativity, but always make sure that your content is relevant to your audience. Pinterest pages can also be used as landing pages for email campaigns, events, or presentations. The boards provide a unique way of organizing content to be visually appealing to your prospects.

Make sure that you are including a good content mix in your Pinterest boards. Followers will want to see a combination of business and culture content. Just make that sure all of your content is visually appealing and interesting.

Advertising and Infographics Rule the B2B Marketing Pins

Today, B2B marketers can get tons of great examples of award-winning infographics and advertising campaigns on Pinterest. When pinning, pin the most visually interesting aspect of what you are sharing, like a special banner, slide, or cover page, in order to get the most engagement and to make your brand look like it belongs. It's a Great Opportunity for Additional Promotion of B2B Campaigns.

The pinning of handbags and skirts, directly or through fans, is a great way for retailers to socially market their goods, but companies that sell $20k consulting packages or $400k aircraft engines still don't have Pinterest in their marketing plans. Should they? If they care about or spend money on any of the following, then the answer is definitely "yes:"

- SEO – While there are many theories about how the big search engines score social media linking, connecting Pinterest can certainly help your efforts.
- Content—Do you have some interesting content that has done well on other social channels? Why not pin it? Just as the Facebook audience is different from the Twitter audience, Pinterest allows you to appeal to a more visually focused crowd that may not be spending their slow hours on Facebook or Twitter.
- Design—Are you a design forward company? Do you typically develop design-forward campaigns? Pinterest is all about the visual, so leverage the fact that graphic designers are one of the most prolific groups of pinners; get your creative team to pin their work to inspire others and themselves!
- Marketing – Just as designers pin and re-pin designs that inspire them, marketers pin and re-pin campaigns that inspire

them. Start a company board to show your peers the beauty of your marketing, and build your reputation among prospects and possible job candidates as a top tier marketing company. Next, start a board with pins of others' marketing campaigns that inspire you.

Get Followed: SEO is Important

Pinterest's search is mainly how people find you and your pins, and it is all about keywords. For example, a picture of a fish with no description will not be found in a search for "fish." However, simply adding a description (Adjectives help!) will immediately get eyes on your pin. Load up relevant, popular keywords in the description of your pins and boards, and you are guaranteed to get more views/ likes/follows.

Fresh Content Creates the Most Waves

Just like any other social media platform, Pinterest rewards those who bring fresh content. So, while it's very easy to fill a board with re-pins, ultimately, the fastest way to increase your followership is by pinning new and interesting items.

Instagram

Instagram is a photo sharing app that can have some relevance to the B2B market, especially with Facebook's recent acquisition of the application. Having more than 27 million users, Instagram has a very active user base. Use Instagram for capturing events and office culture photos. You can also leverage the application to run contests and scavenger hunts.

The Four Stages of Instagram for B2B Curate

Before you begin snapping photos and engaging viewers, it's up to you to create a plan to help you curate fans of your company. Ask questions like these:

- What does my target audience want to see?
- How can I get them to engage with my photos?
- What will get them talking about my company?

At its core, the curate stage is about determining what will make your fans engage with your brand in a positive manner and creating a plan of execution.

Snap

The time has come to start snapping photos! Consider the following objectives as you create your visual content:

- Make it exclusive: Post images that can only be seen on Instagram.
- Make it visually engaging: Instragram users are savvy and creative, and they know a lackluster photo when they see one. Don't post a photo unless it has aesthetic appeal.
- Make it personal: Post photos of your employees at work, to give viewers and potential customer's personal insight into the inner workings of your company. Viewers want to feel like they are part of something, and this type of inside glimpse works wonders.

Hashtag

The Instagram hashtag is a powerful feature to engage your viewers. Hashtags act as keywords, providing a way for people to find photos through a simple search. Hashtags are especially useful as you seek to establish your brand as an industry leader and get more followers. Implement hashtags that are unique to your brand and industry, as well as hashtags that are popular keywords, and remember to use hashtags on all of your posts.

Engage

Engagement with potential customers and sharing are the primary reasons to utilize a platform such as Instragram. Luckily, there are a variety of ways for B2B companies to do this:

- Events: Post photos of events you host for your current and potential clients.
- Geolocation: Use the geolocation feature to provide yet another point of engagement with your viewers.
- Gamification: Hold a contest for your audience. Have viewers submit photos, provide captions, or solve a puzzle about your photos.

Graphics & Dimensions:

Use the correct image dimensions for your social profiles and posts.

Pay attention to the dimensions of the images you are uploading and sharing. If you don't, your images could end up with terrible cropping or distorting. This also applies to your business's social media cover photos.

An easy way to make sure you are displaying your social profiles correctly is to follow the recommended image dimensions for each. Keep in mind that each of these measurements is listed in pixels. Here is a list of dimensions for you to follow for Facebook, Twitter, LinkedIn, Google+, and YouTube.

While the images dimensions are here, check out my website for the infographic.

www.SpiceGirlofTampaBay.com/Book-Gifts

Password: AbundantBlessing

Facebook
- Cover photo: 851 x 315

- Profile Picture: 180 x 180

- App Icons: 111 x 74

- Timeline: 504 x height is up to you for a shared image; 484 x 252 (shared link)

- News Feed: 470 x 394 for a shared image,;470 x 246 for a shared link

Twitter
- Header Image: 1252 x 626

- Profile Picture: 250 x 250

- Image in Feed: 1024 x 512

LinkedIn
- Banner image: 624 x 220

- Logo: 100 x 60

- Link Thumbnail: 100 x 100

Google+
- Cover Photo: 1010 x 608

- Profile Picture: 250 x 250

- Image Post: 800 x 600 (minimum)

Pinterest
- Board Cover: 217 x 147

- Preview Image: 51 x 51

YouTube
- Banner Image: 2560 x 423 (desktop); 1546 x 423 (mobile)

When & How Often to Post to Social Media

There is a ton of information about when you should post on social media sites, but here's the real story. While there hasn't been any singular agreed-upon schedule (Thank God for that!), can you imagine how annoying it would be if every business was posting all at the same time on all social media platforms, there are some guidelines we can follow to make the most of our posts:

Twitter – 10 times per day, from 1:00 am to 10:00 pm Eastern Time, never more than once per hour; seven times per day on weekends, from 3:00 am to 9:00 pm, roughly every three hours

Facebook - two times per day, seven days a week; in the morning between 5:00 am – 6:00 am; in the evening between 3:30 pm – 6:30 pm

LinkedIn - once per day, 7:15 am – 9:30 am; no weekends

Google+ - twice per day; in the morning between 7:00 am – 9:00 am; in the evening between 7:30 pm – 9:30 pm; no weekends

If you are connecting to a global audience, then you should use the schedule above, but keep in mind that you may need to tweet at 3:00 am, since three in the morning Central Time, is 9:00 am in London. If you don't have a global audience, you might not get the same value out of tweeting in the middle of the night.

Flirting with the Fine Art of Frequency

Every time a commercial comes on and is then repeated until you can sing their jingle by heart, that brand has found the delicate balance between annoying the audience and wiggling their way into you mind so that you are walk around singing that jingle and can imagine that commercial.

Social media marketers from big companies face the same challenge. We want to connect with fans and convince them to hit that like button and receive our notifications without driving them away. We aim for the perfect balance of sharing and listening. The truth is that we all end up guessing a lot, trying and testing new combinations on what works and what doesn't.

Get comfortable with guessing; it is required for finding that sweet spot of optimal frequency that fits your audience's needs. However, we can begin by making educated guesses, rather than haphazardously making random choices.

Strike the balance between informative and annoying.

How often do you share content? I am looking to find the balance being informative and being annoying. The continual search to find the sweet spot of "informative" versus "annoying" is the heart of why businesses care about posting frequency at all. We all want to deliver value, but we don't want to go overboard. That being said, where's the fine line?

The Optimal Frequency for Posting on Social Media

To know the absolute BEST posting frequencies is impossible, but we are shooting for optimal results. You can only predict and measure what you do because it involves people, and people love to change their minds and be spontaneous, and while some things about consumer behavior used to be predictable, we are still dealing with humans, and we're not driving the decisions as we were in advertising before social media. We are only creating an environment to essentially be the "life of the party."

- Predict.
- Measure.
- Repeat.

There aren't very many shortcuts here, but with the right data, we can at least gain a head start on the prediction process. Saying beyond a shadow of a doubt that X is the best number of times to post to Twitter, and Y is the best number of times to post to Facebook, would be misleading. There is well-researched data, for sure, but consider it as just a starting point for customizing your own optimal schedule.

When a brand posts twice a day, those posts only receive 57% of the likes and 78% of the comments per post. The drop-off continues as more posts are made in the day.

However, Track Social went a step further to see the effect that multiple posts per day had on a page's total responses in a given day. In this instance, there was no significant change, as post frequency increased. This suggests that you won't lose out on conversations if you increase how often you post.

There is one caveat: Most of this research comes from before Facebook's recent algorithm change. These days, the feed values fresh content highly. As a result, media companies can post four to ten times more often than brands and still see engagement. An Edgerank Checker study posted on the Moz blog determined that one way to counteract the algorithm change might be to publish more frequently, as often as you have fresh, compelling content to share.

Specifically, it depends on what you want to measure. The engagement-per-tweet measure can tell you at what point your individual tweets reach their maximum performance levels. Track Social found this to be a similar number to Social Bakers. Per Track Social, responses per tweet peak at five and then drop off.

Also, consider the incredibly short life cycle of a post. It takes 18 minutes for a tweet to be "over the hill." Facebook posts reach their half-life at the 90-minute mark, nearly four times longer than Twitter.

Bottom line: <u>The first couple of hours are the most important time for your tweet</u>. Schedule your posts when your audience is online. Advice for Google+ is a little more of a stretch. Even heavy users of the service can differ on the "right" frequency.

Frequency and scheduling go hand-in-hand in so many ways in your social media marketing strategy that it's difficult to plan one without the other.

The Late-Night Infomercial Effect

There is, as you might imagine, a flip side to scheduling your posts when your audience is online. We'll call it the Late-Night Infomercial Effect -- another fun tidbit from Peter Bray. It goes a little something like this:

When there's nothing else on, you're more likely to watch an infomercial. When there's little else being tweeted, your tweets are more likely to stand out.

Certain email marketing statistics follow a similar line of thinking. You can see greater open rates and clickthroughs when your email is one of the only ones in the inbox. The data below suggests that the time frame between 8:00 pm. and midnight gets the highest openings and clicks. The same could be said for social media. Maybe posting on off hours isn't all that bad after all!

Furthermore, always be testing, experimenting, iterating, and improving. The line between informative and annoying may be super slim, but it's one that you can find easily with a little practice.

Know Where to Post

Where you should post depends on *where* and *who* your audience is. There are many platforms, and one may be super popular, but is it where your audience is located? If your audience is on Facebook, great. If not, however, it will do little good to post your fantastic content there.

LinkedIn is business-related and not for the cat pictures of Facebook. You'll get slapped around by the users like a rag doll.

Twitter is largely used by customer service departments of big companies, as well as celebrities. So, while you might not like it, that matters little if you want to reach your audience and this is where they are.

Facebook is still the leading social media network, and it continues to grow. It's great for pictures and videos. This is where you can post your cat pics and videos.

Google+ seems to be more casual venting, Q&A, and a platform that people are using because Google says you have to. But 2015, for me, will determine how long it sticks around.

YouTube is the 2nd largest search engine in the world. You can find practically any How-To Video. If you don't have a How-To Video get crakin'! Many companies have taken advantage of this by releasing their ads or marketing campaigns on YouTube first, before they debut on TV.

Pinterest & Instagram are picture based social sites and growing quickly with infographics and all things visual.

Some social media networks have a **more active user-base than others**, a busy social network isn't great if your audience doesn't visit the site. Some statistical research shows that more than 95% of Facebook users log into their accounts every day, while Twitter is 60%, and for LinkedIn, it is 30%. My question for 2015 will be how much of this is desktop at home versus the busy professional on the go and mobile. 2015 will show us all the way.

Social Media Management Tools – Simplicity For You

While we are managing your social media, it's important to be educated in social media tools themselves. So the number one challenge for the business professional is time management. It's no wonder that there are tools to help better manage your time on social media as well.

Automation

Do's & Don'ts

Automation of your social media marketing can help you become significantly more productive in your day. However, a word of warning here is that you can only automate your social media presence to a certain point. Find that delicate balance of being present while staying in the conversation with your audience. Here are some amazing tools to choose from (hint: my favorite is on top)

- HootSuite
  https://hootsuite.com
- Buffer
  https://bufferapp.com
- Sendible
  http://sendible.com/

When I worked in corporate America, automation was a huge part of what I did and what I implemented. I used a Franklin Planner (yes, I know that is dating me), and I just followed my schedule to get the day done. Automation has been a big part of my life for as long as I can remember. I love to find helpful ways to work smarter—anything to shave an extra few minutes off my day and, quite honestly, make me look totally organized, even when I am not… I'm all in!

I am always interested in making things better, faster, and easier, so out of curiosity, I researched and tested many platforms that offer social media automation and came up with a couple of winners: Hootsuite and Buffer.

Social media marketing does not begin and end with automation alone. Automation is one tool that you should use to better impact your affectivity. This means that you can use automation to get more done on a long-term basis, because you save a couple of hours per month setting up a planned schedule.

Based on our discussion so far, you know where I am going. You need pan. You need a strategy. So, let's go over some basics to achieve social media automation that is both efficient and engaged:

Have a plan, and work the plan.

Know when to post to make the most impact. This means actually reading the insights to know the most effective way to get your brand name out there.

Don't post the same content on all the same platforms all the time! Most likely, your audience and raving fans are subscribed everywhere you are. If you overwhelm them with the same content over and over again, you'll quickly wear them out.

Imagine social media automation to be more like drinking water. You do drink liquids automatically when your thirsty, and sometimes you have to intentionally remind yourself that water – plain water – is healthier, and you purposefully drink plain water for a short period of time before you forget about it again.

Automation of social media is best used when you apply that analogy. Use it, and set it up once a month for the rest of the month; purposefully spend the rest of the month checking on the progress. Maybe you prepare the next batch, or maybe when a great idea strikes, you sprinkle in a few nuggets throughout the month. You remain engaged from beginning to end. This should be the case for ALL of your social media accounts.

Automate what you can, and remain engaged on a consistent basis. With proper use of social media automation, you can make your time spent on your social media online marketing as productive and profitable as possible.

Automation and conversation go together like peanut butter and jelly. The quicker you understand that, the more you truly work to build an efficient, effective process. Here are four simple steps to starting your automation plan:

- Understand when to automate and when to engage.
- Choose your tools for automation.
- Find your ideal automation schedule.
- Create ways to stay tuned in to the conversation.

Step 1: Understand when to automate.

It's important to resist the temptation; not everything should be automated. Even the big guys struggle with understanding when and how to walk the fine line of automation and engagement.

Avoid automating things like responses to users as a strategy to engage. They know you are delivering value not on their time, but on your own, and as such, you'll turn them off quickly.

Here are some ideas about when you'll find it best to schedule ahead of time and when it is best to do the work manually:

- Automate your Content Curation

Finding and sharing great content online is a useful way to build a brand and an audience on social media. Automation helps this process in two ways: It provides a means of posting these updates at the best times for your audience, whether you're around or not, and it frees you up to have more time to find amazing content to share.

What's a good rule of thumb for content sharing? You'll likely find a golden ratio for your particular audience based on your social analytics, but if you're in the mood for experimenting, here's an interesting one I found: The 5-3-2 rule of social media sharing, proposed by TA McCann states that for every ten updates you post, to a social media channel, the following should be true:

- 5 should be content from others, relevant to your audience

- 3 should be content from you, relevant to your audience—and not a sales pitch

- 2 should be personal, non-work related content that helps humanize you and/or your brand

- 5-3-2 rule of content sharing

The result of maintaining a schedule like this leads you to focus on your audience more than on yourself. In that sense, the system is better explained as a way to ensure that you stay on point with your marketing; whether you follow it to a T is less important as whether or not you're maintaining the right message.

Automate your non-urgent social media posts.

Beyond content curation, most social media users will find themselves sharing thoughts, quotes, re-tweets, and more through their networks of choice. You could imagine these being the "personal" notes in the 5-3-2 rule mentioned above. Provided these posts are not time-sensitive, these would make perfect sense to automate and schedule.

Headline Testing

Automation ensures that we can complete this process all at once, rather than popping in and out every few hours when it's time to post again.

Automate your marketing flows.

Many big businesses have flows and funnels that begin with social media—lead capture from tweets, product improvements from social suggestions, troubleshooting, feedback, and more. If it makes sense to you, automate these to cut down on the work it takes to manage these social accounts. For instance, if you can trigger a lead-generating process each time you 'favorite' a tweet, you've made the job that much easier!

Do NOT automate customer interactions.

Many busy companies might be tempted to automate simple responses, such as a thank-you, but anything more than that is a dangerous game. Plus, customers appreciate unique and individual responses on social media, and many of them love social media as much as they do because of these interactions specifically. When you take the human aspect out of social media, it isn't all that social anymore. Automating customer interactions might never lead to such bad press as was seen with Progressive, but it can have damaging effects on engagement and reputation nonetheless. Customers can tell when they're dealing with an assembly line instead of a human.

Do NOT automate troubleshooting.

In a similar vein, troubleshooting should generally be left to real people and real interactions. There may be opportunities to streamline communication if there is a common problem that can be fixed with a simple answer, but even then, it is best to always run it by a human first. When the customer is already inconvenienced by a problem with your product, it makes things that much worse to compound the problems with a robotic response.

Step 2: Choose your automation tools.

HootSuite

HootSuite is a social media management system for businesses and organizations that collaboratively executes campaigns across multiple social networks from one secure, web-based dashboard. Key social network integrations include Facebook, Twitter, LinkedIn, and Google+, as well as a suite of social content apps for YouTube, Flickr, Instagram, Yammer, Tumblr, and more.

In late 2013 - early 2014, HootSuite hit 5 million users, including 79 of the Fortune 100 companies. Along with HootSuite's web platform, 20% of users access the dashboard through their mobile devices, including iPhone, Android, Blackberry, and iPad. HootSuite also offers localized versions of their dashboard in 12 languages - English, French, Italian, Japanese, German, Spanish, Portuguese, Chinese Traditional, Chinese Simplified, Dutch, Polish, and Indonesian.

There are many benefits to HootSuite Pro.

Engage: Optimize your audience engagement by creating search streams, scheduling messages, and monitoring all of your social network profiles from one customizable web and mobile dashboard.

Collaborate: Invite clients and colleagues to participate in your social media management. Assign messages for follow up and share streams, helping you increase efficiency.

Analyze: Measure your efforts, using over 40 social analytics modules to build and share custom reports. Alternatively, select from one of our pre-made templates for quick and easy reporting.

Secure: Share access with team members without compromising security. The team permission levels and advanced sharing options ensure that you remain in control of your valuable social profiles and accounts.

Buffer

Organize your social sharing with Buffer.

Buffer lets you connect your Twitter, Facebook, Google+, and LinkedIn accounts, so that you can create queues of content that are sent/posted at pre-specified times. Tools like this are incredibly helpful for automating social sharing and content curation, as you can place all of your good finds here, and let Buffer handle the rest. Try the Buffer browser extension for a truly supercharged experience. Buffer a re-tweet.

Connect your apps with IFTTT and Zapier.

Tools like IFTTT and Zapier are heaven-sent for automation. These services connect apps with one another to create a call-and-response chain of action. For instance, you can connect your blog's RSS feed and your Twitter, Facebook, G+ and LinkedIn accounts, so that every time you publish a new post, your social account gets updated as well. And that's just the tip of the iceberg!

Both options allow you to browse their long lists of possibilities, so you are sure to find something useful. Potential recipes include automated systems for favoriting tweets and sending them to Buffer, archiving to Dropbox whenever you are tagged in a Facebook photo, and saving articles to read later, directly from favorite social media posts. Here is how the process might look if you were to connect your IFTTT with your blog:

Klout

The Klout website launched in 2008 and while relatively new on the scene, this website and mobile app uses social media analytics to rank registered users according to online social influence via the "Klout Score", between 1 and 100. Klout measures the size of a user's social media network and correlates the content created to measure how other users interact with that content. While it's primary analytics are based in Twitter, they do include several social media platforms: Facebook, Google+, LinkedIn, and Instagram.

I don't buy into the algorithm used on this platform as being solid and unbiased, but it does provide a valuable service. Content curation. That is use of other's peoples content

Klout is a popular platform for those who are content-deficient. It is very common to get writers block.

Sendible

Sendible is a social media management, monitoring & analytics platform that helps companies manage their social media presence more efficiently. This platform allows users to send not only bulk emails but bulk SMS messages as well. This platform is similar to Hootsuite in management ways in that it allows multiple streams to be viewed, managed and ROI measured in one location.

I can't honestly write much about Sendible, I've been there and done that. I moved into Hootsuite. So go for the trial and make your own decision on which is best for your style!

Step 3: Create a system for staying in the conversation.

Just the fact that you are performing this step in the process is a good sign. Desiring to stay in the conversation will be beneficial for whatever system you end up installing.

Use Mention to track yourself and your brand on social media.

Mention is a super-powered version of Google Alerts that you can use to track your name across websites, blogs, and social media channels. Mention searches and finds any instance whatsoever in which you or your brand is mentioned, and you can reply and engage straight from the Mention dashboard. Like with Google Alerts, you can be updated via email when you receive a Mention; I've opted for a daily email to bring me up-to-speed on who's saying what. It's a hand-delivered opportunity for personal engagement with an audience.

Twitter, Facebook, and the like have the capability to notify you of virtually anything that happens involving your account. Oftentimes, these notification settings are one of the first things users turn off, especially once the scope of emails becomes apparent. I'm not suggesting that you opt-in to every single email from your social media channels, but it's definitely worth a look to see which alerts and notifications might be helpful.

For instance, I have chosen to be notified for almost everything Twitter-related, as I seek to build relationships there. From the list of options, I've only turned off the notification for new followers, and even with that, I check the list daily in order to reciprocate those who have followed.

Step 4: Set aside time to dive into the stream and engage.

Of course, the best way to stay in the stream of social media conversation is to roll up your pant legs and wade on in.

One way to do this is to schedule a block of time each day to visit your social media profiles. At Buffer, we lovingly call this the "drive-by." You can use this time any number of different ways to engage with your community. Respond to comments, post spontaneously, engage in what others are posting, etc. Since automation is saving you time with posting, you should have a little extra time to make a drive-by one of your daily habits.

Time Management is a challenge for anyone, however in social media don't look directly into the streams…it's too easy to get wrapped up in all the videos and pictures just like what you are doing. {smile}. You are there for business, use your tools to manage your time and be effective. Use your personal time to check everyone else out.

Avoid the pitfalls of automation.

Beyond the four-step process for a social media automation strategy, there are a few other best practices to be aware of when it comes to scheduling and automating your online presence.

Customize your messages for different networks.

As you're crafting your content queue, remember who's on the other end of all this work: your audience. What's best for them?

You may find that, on Twitter, it is best to be brief, whereas Google+ users enjoy a lengthier message.

Different styles work better on different networks. Why not aim for distinct messages for each of the social networks you share? Have one style for Twitter, another for Facebook, another for Google+, etc.

Simply plugging in set messages to be spread across all your social media platforms can sometimes look insincere and robotic. However, if a user sees how much thought you place into creating unique messages across different platforms, imagine what an impression it could make!

Don't schedule too far in advance.

The goal with automation is to fill your queue so that you can focus your energy elsewhere—finding great content to share, responding to customers' needs, brainstorming new ways to take over the world, etc.

Be careful not to schedule too far out in advance. Doing so might lead to your missing/forgetting the message behind your sharing. You could end up with untimely content that made sense two weeks earlier, but doesn't on the day it goes live. Schedule your posts for a week or so out, but by all means, dive in daily for spontaneous updates as you see fit.

Stay abreast of current events.

When automating, it's important to be aware of what's going on in the world around you. The Hurricane Sandy example is probably the most recent instance in which current events dramatically changed the context for thousands of social media users. Another good example—in a positive way—is that of Oreo and its response to the power outage during the Super Bowl.

Be prepared to hit the pause button.

When big news does strike, it's important to be prepared to hit pause on all your automation instances. Buffer lets you tick off the days you want to stop your posts, and similar scheduling programs also allow for a full scale halt if the situation requires it.

Takeaways

Hopefully you see the advantages of automation and the symbiotic relationship automation has with conversation. One cannot be as effective without the other. Automation benefits from conversation, because you have a more engaged group of followers. Conversation benefits from automation because you are freed to spend more time engaging with those who matter.

Begin by figuring out what is best to automate, and be sure to end with a good balance of scheduling and conversing. While it might be easiest to automate it all, you'll find that being part of the conversation will pay higher dividends in the long run.

Demographics and Your Audience

Each social media platform has a unique identity based on who uses the network and how they're engaging on the site. LinkedIn has developed a special identity — and utility — as the social network for professionals. However, it has come a long way from when it was simply a forum to make your resume visible to employers and your job postings searchable for recruitment.

Engagement is rising quickly on LinkedIn, as the social network becomes a content destination. The social network is also highly profitable and highly esteemed among the professional community, and it has a big international presence. These factors will make LinkedIn increasingly compelling to marketers. Already, a survey from Cogent Research finds that LinkedIn is the preferred social network by a wide margin for building a brand identity.

Being able to identify the demographics of social media audiences at a granular level is the basis for all targeted marketing and messaging. The report also spotlights the opportunities that lie ahead for each social network, as well as how social media usage compares between the U.S. and international markets.

Here is where some of the biggest opportunities lie on the major networks:

Facebook's users skew younger, and that means that brands that advertise luxury goods and services are still finding more success advertising in magazines than on social media. Other types of brands, such as fast-moving consumer goods, do perform well on Facebook.

Additionally, Facebook users show high ad engagement overall, accounting for half of all retargeted clicks on the Web.

People tend to use Twitter for news consumption. In 2012, 83% of users reported seeing news on Twitter. Additionally, bulks of users are located in urban areas. For brands, the best time to post on Twitter is Monday through Thursday, between 1 p.m. and 3 p.m. The worst time is after 3 p.m. on a Friday.

LinkedIn has the advantage of being the place for white-collar professionals to network, meaning its population is highly desirable, since it has a high-income, highly educated user base. The best time to post on LinkedIn is Tuesday through Thursday, when professionals are either beginning or finishing their workdays.

Pinterest is riding the wave of mobile. It's really the breakout tablet-first social network. Pinterest users already account for 48.2% of all social media sharing on iPads. They're primarily sharing food and drink-related content, as well as family and parenting-related items. Pinterest is poised to become one of the top four social networks.

Over 90% of people who use Instagram are under the age of 35, which makes it an attractive platform for the many apparel, entertainment, and media brands focused on the 18- to 34-year-old age bracket.

Tumblr is strong with teens and young adults interested in self-expression. What's more, the teens who do use Tumblr use it often. 61% of 13- to 18-year-olds said they used the service several hours a week or more, according to a study conducted by Y Combinator Partner Gerry Tan.

12 Social Media Mistakes Companies Make

Social media can be a powerful marketing tool. Used the wrong way, however, these social media sites can deliver predictably negative impacts on your business. So, how can you create a positive impression of your business and/or products on popular social media sites, such as Facebook, Twitter, LinkedIn, and Google+, while avoiding potentially costly social media blunders? Here are my top 12 picks for the most common social media mistakes businesses make and how to avoid them.

- **Not Knowing that it's Social + Search**
  It's not one or the other! It's both…at the same time! Everything you do on the Internet is there to stay, so make it work! Find your keywords, and use them in your social media postings. Later, we'll be going over some tools and tricks to help keep you on track.

- **Not having a social media policy.**
  It's your business and your reputation; you need to be clear on how everyone who works for you – both contractors and employees – are to represent themselves online. If you are not specific and clear with them, you leave it up to them to determine what THEY think is best, and it could lead to potential problems later.

- **Treating all social media sites as if they are the same.**
  Social Media is not a one-size-fits-all strategy. There are pieces of content that can be the same across all sites, but the

verbiage is ifferent. For example, a long message on Facebook can be up to 450 words of uber-casual entertainment; Twitter messaging is 140 characters of straight-to-the-point talk; LinkedIn requires a different more professional language, and most fields are best when fewer than 250 characters are used.

Many businesses simultaneously blast the exact same message across Facebook, Twitter, Google+, LinkedIn, etc., not realizing that this comes across as fake, impersonal, or spam-like.

- **Using social media as a megaphone.**

Social media is self-explanatory: Its purpose is for a user to socialize with others in an effort to get them to know, likes, and trust you and who you are. If you are using the megaphone approach, that typically means you aren't allowing anyone to get close enough to you to accomplish that, both on social media and in real life. Engagement builds loyalty, and loyalty translates to sales.

- **Focusing on quantity of followers instead of quality.**

Having a fan page of 1,000,000 people who couldn't give a crap about what you have to say isn't converting anyone into a raving fan. You might as well go and talk to a wall. It would be that engaging. In all honesty, why are you out there working to get new customers, hoping they will buy your product or service, only to talk to the wall instead of to people who really want to listen to and talk with you. You don't want to waste your time and efforts, so why focus solely on the numbers? It is far better to have 100 fans who are talking with and about you than 1,000,000 who couldn't care less.

- **Posting inappropriate content.**

    At one time, I thought that content of a colorful nature would be necessary, but I was wrong. So, here is my recommendation. If your grandma's mouth would drop to the floor and her teeth fall out after viewing your post, don't post it. It'll take practice, but I promise that you'll quickly find out what turns your audience on and what turns them off. If you don't know what they want, ask them!

- **Not monitoring social media for suggestions, complaints, or questions.**

    Customers are talking about you online, whether you like it or not. Ask any marketer, or anyone who knows you, for that matter. You can avoid negative repercussions of social media by being there and using it. Your customers expect you to be present and to be listening. If no one is listening or acknowledging customer posts, customers assume you don't care.

- **Deleting or ignoring negative comments – or responding in kind.**

    Keep cool, and stay professional. It's not personal. Its business, and it is totally bogus to believe that any company is so golden that no one ever complains about it. You just have to get over it. You're not that good…no one is. We have all had our fair share of negative press. What matters is what you do with it, how you respond to it, and how you change your future actions based on the feedback. It is always best to apologize (even if you haven't done anything wrong), and offer to contact the person by email to work out the problem. A simple acknowledgment of a problem can prevent a potential PR nightmare.

- **Not knowing when to post.**
  There is a ton of information about when you should post on social media sites, in the end what works best is what is best for your audience. There are some great guidelines and I'm going to be giving you those outlined just a bit later.

- **Posting too infrequently or over-posting.**
  Social media marketing requires patience and persistence. You can't post once in a while – whether that is once a month or once a year – and expect people to come flocking to your door to buy your products/services. You need to post five to seven days a week, every week, every month, and consistently.

- **Overusing hashtags.**
  If you are not even sure what a hashtag is, great! You're not doing this one. If you do use hashtags, keep in mind that using more than three is over-doing it. #NoOne #Pays #Attention to #This. #JustStopIt. Hashtags are meant to group a conversation in a 'room,' so that it is easier to have group conversations. Having a conversation with multiple hashtags is nearly impossible. The other implication is that

you want your post to be viewed by others who are using that hashtag in their conversations. Okay, you party crasher, you! #JustStopIt. #GetOverYourself.

- **Not including a measurable call-to-action in social media posts.**

  People need to be told what to do. This means that you need to include links to the resources, and tell them what you need them to do. "Call Today." "Click Here." You'll find that I always offer loads of resources and tell you where to go, how to get there, and what you need to do once you get there. Now, stop laughing. I know the image that just flashed into your mind. And while I would definitely tell you where to get off the train, this is a #JustDoItMoment.

Content

Know Content & Strategies Work

Content Strategies – Where to Find More When I Have None!

Use Compelling Content. Generating consistently compelling content is key to your social media presence and gaining Fans and followers. It takes time, effort, and requires tapping into your expertise and resources.

RSS & Blogs

Including a RSS to your blog's website will increase web traffic and draw in new customers. The blog is to focus on providing How-To instructions to the Do-It-Yourselfers. Giving information away to the Do-It-Yourselfers along with a "list of items necessary" will increase you audience's view of you as expert in the industry. Consistency is necessary to maintain the audience confidence.

An RSS dubbed Really Simple Syndication is an automatic feed service. This service allows your website to easily circulate information to a wide number of people. RSS is a powerful marketing technique as it gets your message to visitors who have chosen to subscribe to your site. Search engines put a lot of emphasis on fresh content, and the RSS feed is constantly generating new content that is picked up by the search engines, which therefore will increase your ranking.

Press Releases, Article Writing, & Syndication

A **press release**, **news release**, **media release**, **press statement** or **video release** is a written or recorded communication directed at members of the news media for the purpose of announcing something supposedly newsworthy. Typically, they are mailed, faxed, or e-mailed to assignment editors at newspapers, magazines, radio stations, television stations, or television networks.

Websites have changed the way press releases are submitted. Commercial, fee-based press release distribution services, such as news wire services, or free website services co-exist, making news distribution more affordable and leveling the playing field for smaller businesses when you don't have a one on one relationship with the editor already. Such websites hold a repository of press releases and claim to make a company's news more prominent on the web and searchable via major search engines.

The use of press releases is common in the field of public relations (PR) for mass reach but not a great choice for a local reach. Typically, the aim is to attract favorable media attention to the PR professional's client and/or provide publicity for products or events marketed by those clients.

A press release provides reporters with an information subsidy containing the basics needed to develop a news story. Press releases can announce a range of news items, such as scheduled events, personal promotions, awards, new products and services, sales and other financial data, accomplishments, etc. They are often used in generating a feature story or are sent for the purpose of announcing news conferences, upcoming events or a change in corporation. Uncritical use or overuse of press releases by journalists has been dubbed "churnalism".

<u>Plan of Action:</u> Use of a Commercial Press Release Services to increase link wheel viability as well as develop long lasting contacts in the media. This process takes time to develop by reaching out to those media connections, but is necessary step.

Email List Management & Newsletters

As a small organization, your passion for what you do and the quality of your customer relationships are what separate you from the big guys. And when you use Email Marketing, you'll be able to reinforce those relationships and connect with your customers in a way no one else can—every single time you hit 'Send.'

Email Marketing delivers bottom-line results. While there are several you can partner with, use one that fits your budget as well as your technical skill level. As a company, we partner with Constant Contact Email Marketing System, but use the system that makes the most sense to you. This system offers you a fast, effective way to get your message out to customers and keep your organization visible and on the top of their minds. It's a breakthrough marketing tool that's just as easy to use as it is powerful. But it doesn't end there.

There are custom built social media tools included in the Constant Contact Platform as well as over 400+ email templates. So now, when you send an email to your mailing list, you'll be able to connect with a whole new audience of potential customers via social media sites—and generate even more new business.

The ability to communicate with your customers, past, present and future is perhaps the most valuable aspect of web based marketing. Spam (unwelcome email) is perhaps the most negative aspect of email based marketing. An email database properly managed is the best and least expensive way to reach your growing customer base. Whether you're sending out a monthly newsletter, special offer, or an update on your business notifying your customers via email is the quickest, most cost effective environmentally responsible and universal way to stay in contact with your customers.

To demonstrate the potential and magnitude of a well-managed email capture and an email database management program we present the following example: If a business were to collect 20 email addresses per day from its customers and an additional 20 per day from potential customers viewing the business' website, you would establish a qualified list of individuals (that wish to be contacted by you) of 14,600 a year or 43,800 in three years. If you were to use this database monthly to notify these customers of a special promotion and only 1% respond to it, this would translate into 438 additional sales / walk-in traffic each month. Just imagine being able to effect sales and / or walk in traffic to your business with a simple e-mail to your past customers.

<u>Plan of Action:</u> Integration of Constant Contact or some other email marketing system and launch a monthly campaign that helps keep your brand in front of the potential clients who know you and increases memory retention when it comes time for those longer decision makers to make a buying decision. Adding that Call-to-Action to your website.

Promotions, Daily Deals & Coupons

Daily Deals and Coupons are a very popular source for drawing traffic; careful consideration must be given to include products and /or services that make good business sense. The deals published where your audience is will attract more new customers as well as create more brand awareness about your business, however don't overreach for brand awareness to fall short with your cash flow to get there.

Deals can focus on excess inventory, would be a great avenue to generate new walk-in traffic and increase visibility into the community. An entire campaign focused on the medical community needs to be developed...if it makes sense.

Several great resources for businesses are available for use. Check out the sites and talk with them to determine the best fit, if any is right for your business.

Here are a few to get you started, there are more out there, but start with the ones whose emailing list of interested buyers already is nurtured and waiting for deals online.

- Your Current Customer Base Deals – Use Deal Promotion Tools in your email marketing system such as Constant Contact
- Amazon Local - http://local.amazon.com/merchants
- Groupon – http://groupon.com
- Living Social - https://www.livingsocial.com/

Social Reviews

Unless you've been living under a rock for the past 3 years, you'd notice a very big trend on the web--social bookmark and media websites have become "all that" on the web. Yelp, Google+, Facebook, StumbleUpon, Trip Advisor; any of these popular sites sound familiar?

This is where a lot of social review traffic will originate. In essence, these sites are driven and "controlled" by the users. Users or members choose which content they want to review and bookmark, and this will lead into viewing and discussing of the site bookmarked, the products and services as well as the content. Sites such as these are immensely popular, and flow traffic that the average website owner can only ever imagine having. That's a lot of traffic, isn't it? But is it really useful?

Review sites are generally supported by advertising. Some business review sites may also allow businesses to pay for enhanced listings, which doesn't affect the reviews and ratings but does allow for the listing to be viewed more often than other listing. This is especially helpful when an enhanced listing shows up on a competitors listing and it's not so good. Product review sites may be supported by providing affiliate links to the websites that sell the reviewed items.

With the growing popularity of affiliate programs on the Internet, a new sort of review site has emerged - the affiliate product review site. This type of site is usually professionally designed and written to maximize conversions, and is used by e-commerce marketers. It's often based on a blog platform like WordPress, has a privacy and contact page to help with SEO, and has commenting and interactivity turned off. It will also have an e-mail gathering device in the form of an opt-in, or drop-down list to help the aspiring e-commerce business person build an e-mail list to market to.

Reviews are your reputation online and it's not just that the reviews need to all be good. Because no business is golden all the time. We all have hiccups and bumps in the road. It's how you respond to those bits of bad reviews. A word of caution though, if your audience is all negative, listen to them. They are angry, yes and sometimes just plain hurtful. But if you improve in the areas that they are complaining about and thank them for making you better, you'll make more friends from it than anything else you do.

Summary

This is the best advice I have ever received. They are three simple truths that I use to live by.

1. Be thankful where you are at and for having achieved that level already. You will never grow past your personal gladness.
2. Just do it and stop Thinking about it!
3. Put it in a list and move through it. Do the hard stuff first when you have a hard time figuring out where to start. Get it out of the way and safe the easy or fun stuff for later.

The best tool, I saved this so long ago that I have no idea where I got it. It's not original, but it is timeless and invaluable.

My Most Important Tool

The most important tool on my desk isn't my laptop, my complicated "What's Next" action list, it's not my phone (on which I spend more time than I like), or even my fancy fountain pen collection. It's my timer…on my iPad.

I work in 50-minute chunks, followed by 10 minutes of goof-off time.

Goof-off time is really important when you're doing creative, difficult work. Your brain needs time to play and rest and have a good time, or it won't work for you when you need it. Sometimes I knit; sometimes I hang out with the cat; sometimes I just walk in circles. Under no circumstances, however, do I do anything productive.

My social media connection time is also on a timer. Twitter is confined to specific times of the day, with no more than ten minutes allotted at once. I usually answer emails in 20-minute chunks.

I don't have enough follow-up time in my day. I do the best I can with the time I have, and sometimes I drop the ball.

It's 2015. Our lives are insanely complex, and our social obligations got overwhelming. We dropped the ball. If you're not doing heart surgery or managing a nuclear power plant, you're allowed to drop the ball. I did.

As bad as I feel when I don't get back to someone, I've also realized that I can choose to spend my energy feeling like a terrible person, or I can choose to spend my energy helping as many people as I can. The latter doesn't just feel better; it also makes a lot more sense. So to those of you who it seems like I have neglected in 2014, I am sorry. Growing up and growing forward is painful at times and there are moments times when we just have to pick ourselves up and move on again.

Index

1

12 Social Media Mistakes Companies Make — 187

3

3 Types of Search Engines — 81

A

Archetype
   Brand Archetype #1: The Sage — 29
   Brand Archetype #10: The Lover — 38
   Brand Archetype #11: The Jester — 39
   Brand Archetype #12: The Regular Guy/Girl — 40
   Brand Archetype #2: The Innocent — 30
   Brand Archetype #3: The Explorer — 31
   Brand Archetype #4: The Ruler — 32
   Brand Archetype #5: The Creator — 33
   Brand Archetype #6: The Caregiver — 34
   Brand Archetype #7: The Magician — 35
Archetypes Explained — 28
Archetytpe
   Brand Archetype #9: The Outlaw — 37
Archeype
   Brand Archetype #8: The Hero — 36

C

Call to Action — 101
Competitive Differentiators And Unique Selling Proposition (USP) — 45
Customers — 64

D

<u>Demographics and Your Audience Engagement Opportunities</u>   185

E

<u>E3 – The Real Power of Social Media</u>   116
    <u>Education</u>   118
    <u>Engagement</u>   117
    <u>Entertainment</u>   116
    <u>Exposure Is Everything</u>   119
<u>Email List Management & Newsletters</u>   198

I

Index   207
Internet Sales Funnel
    Browsers   55
    <u>Consumers</u>   56

K

Keyword
    Definition - What does Keyword mean?   72
Keyword Research, Key Phrases, & Key Word Identification for your
    Specific Market   71

L

Link Building   90
<u>Local Searches - Why, What, How</u>   77
<u>Logo & Graphic Design</u>   43

M

<u>Measurement and Analysis</u>   122
<u>Mobile Marketing</u>   79

O

Online Advertising & Pay Per Click	92

P

Press Releases, Article Writing, & Syndication	196
Promotions, Daily Deals & Coupons	200
Prospects	60

R

Raving Fans	66
RSS & Blogs	195

S

Search Engines Demystified	75
Social Media	111
Flirting with the Fine Art of Frequency	164
Graphics & Dimensions:	161
Know Where to Post	168
When & How Often to Post to Social Media	163
Social Media Channels	
Coordinate Your Social Channels	128
Facebook	134
Google+	140
Instagram	158
Integrate	133
LinkedIn	150
Pinterest	155
Twitter	143
Which One to Choose??	132
Social Media Management Tool	
Automation	170
Social Media Optimization	124
Social Reviews	201

T

Tangible Business Goals	42
Texting - is No Longer Just Enough	121
The Internet Sales Funnel	53

W

Website
Audience	97
Compatibility and Image Restrictions	99
Content	97
Key Issues in Website Design	102
Social Score – Are you connected?	108
Test your keywords.	89
Website Development	97

Websites
Meta Data – Myth or Needed?	88

Y

Your Competition's Business	50
Your Competition's Media Presence	49
Your Ideal Client, Not the Average One	51

www.ingramcontent.com/pod-product-compliance
Lightning Source LLC
Chambersburg PA
CBHW071421170526
45165CB00001B/348